MENTORING HIS WAY

DISCIPLE TWELVE

VOLUME 2

Personal Characteristics
of a Godly Life

DR. ROY L. COMSTOCK

Foreword by
Paul A. Cedar, D.Min./D.D.

Printed in the United States of America
Second edition 2019
Published by Christian Mentors Network, Inc.
24307 Magic Mountain Parkway #208
Valencia, CA 91355

CONTENTS

Discussion questions at the end of each chapter

ACKNOWLEDGMENTS

There are many people that I could acknowledge as having helped me in my journey toward living a more godly life. Though my ministry is primarily with men, it is a woman that has had the greatest impact on my spiritual walk. That woman is my wife, Sarah. She is teaching me how to love and how to give without expecting anything in return; she does it—just for the love of it. Because of her example, I am learning how to love others more than I love myself. I pray that everyone will have the joy of knowing this relationship with their spouse that Sarah and I have. It is not always perfect, but we are both committed to glorifying God in all that we say and do. Thank you, Sarah. I love you with all my heart.

When I first started writing this book in prison, I asked myself this question, "What Biblical values have I compromised that caused me to be where I am and how do I explain to my children how to keep from making the same mistakes?" I want to acknowledge our children Denise, Mike and Michelle their spouses and our beautiful grandchildren for the great contribution they have all made to my life and ministry. It is a real joy to see how God has protected each of them and kept them in close relationship with Himself. I also want to acknowledge my oldest brother, Alex, for standing by me through both the good and the bad times. Thank you all for your love and encouragement.

There are many others that I want to acknowledge without whom, this series of books would not have come to fruition. The graduates of my first training class were fellow inmates at the California Institution for Men. The superintendent and the chaplain gave me permission to lead a Bible study for the men who were permanently assigned to that prison. I wrote the lessons each evening and typed them during the day in the superintendent's office where I worked as a clerk. My friend and fellow inmate Billy Dugger, who I worked with in the office, retyped and edited the material so that it would be readable. At the end of the study we graduated twenty-four inmates. Since then many have completed this three-volume series resulting in transformed lives.

I sent the manuscript home to Sarah and she went over it and gave it to our friend Bob Root. Bob put it in the computer where he formatted it and prepared it for its first release and copyright in 1989. When I rewrote it as a mentoring practicum course for the International Bible Institute (IBI), our daughter-in-law, Ariana, edited the entire manuscript. Our daughter Michelle Beck helped in the rewriting of this Godly Life series. She designed developed a Mentor's Guide for each of the three volumes.

The late Dr. Earle E. Williams, President and Founder of IBI, as my personal mentor and friend for forty years encouraged and enabled me when I needed it most. I want to thank Dr. Paul A. Cedar, Chairman of Mission America Coalition for writing the foreword and for being a faithful friend for over five decades. Dr. Jess Moody, former senior pastor First Baptist Church, Van Nuys, California, came to my office and confronted me and told me that I needed to get my life right with the Lord; he kept coming back until I made that decision. He sent me the following note: "God bless you, Roy. Yours is a great story. Every saint has a past, and every sinner has a future. Keep reaching them for Jesus, my beautiful friend!"

I also want to thank the late Dr. W.P. "Tex" Rutledge, senior pastor of Praise Chapel of Santa Clarita, California, for being the senior mentor in our first mentor/discipler training classes. You will see his invaluable contribution throughout. Last, but not least, are my two friends, Bill Creitz and Patrick Campbell. Both, while participating in the mentor/discipler training classes, and on their own time, put hours into editing and rewriting this material with the hope that lives will be transformed into the "Image of Christ."

Physical Characteristics of a Godly Life

.

FOREWORD

Mentoring is "in." It has become an immensely popular subject in our culture during the past few years. The challenge is that although some people are writing about it and many more are talking about it, there seems to be relatively few who are actually doing it. Jesus believed in mentoring. In fact, He spent the majority of His time during His three years of public ministry mentoring twelve men who He personally chose to be His disciples.

The Apostle Paul also believed in mentoring and he encouraged others to do the same. He instructed Timothy, one of the young men that he mentored, *"And the things you have heard me say in the presence of many witnesses entrust to reliable people who will also be qualified to teach others"* (II Timothy 2:2, NIV). To the believers in Thessalonica Paul wrote, *"On the contrary, we worked night and day, laboring and toiling...in order to make ourselves a model for you to follow"* (II Thessalonians 3:8-9, NIV). Paul presented the ultimate model for mentoring when he wrote, *"Imitate me, just as I also imitate Christ"* (I Corinthians 11:1, NKJV).

Without a doubt, Jesus Christ is the one person who has ever lived who is fully qualified to be a model for living for every one of us. Jesus alone is the ultimate model for our lives. Roy Comstock has come to understand that important truth. In his helpful three-volume series, Roy has identified twelve basic Biblical characteristics of a Godly life. He believes that one living a Godly life mentors automatically. These principles can be of great help to anybody who desires to follow Christ unreservedly and then to help others do the same.

This book has not been written by a perfect man or by one whose life has always been a model for others to follow. Roy's life has not always been easy. He, like all true Christians, has been and is a work of God "in process." We may call this Roy Comstock's "Prison Epistle," since much of this material was written while he was serving a prison term. Roy became a Christian as a teenager after being raised in countless foster homes. He attended two Christian colleges and became successful in business. Roy has a great heart for evangelism, and has been used of God in many ways, including teaching Christian seminars.

At one-point, major failure came into his marriage, his business, and his personal life. The good news is that, instead of departing from the faith, Roy repented and turned to Christ in a deeper way than ever before. He cried out to the Lord concerning his own life, and the Lord responded not only to his needs, but also taught him insights that can be of great help to anyone who desires to follow Jesus Christ. It was during his time in prison that the Lord revealed many of the principles that Roy Comstock calls the "Twelve Characteristics of a Godly Life."

The focus of this three-volume series is upon following Jesus Christ - the One who is the perfect model for all our lives. He is available to be our mentor. The basic principles shared are both Biblical and practical. Volume One has to do with the Spiritual Characteristics, Volume Two is about Personal Characteristics, and Volume Three is concerned with Lifestyle Characteristics.

Together they help the reader to draw nearer to our Lord Jesus and follow Him more faithfully and effectively. As you begin the study of this book, I would encourage you to approach this material with prayer and openness to God. You do not need to agree with all the teaching in order to be helped. Ask our Lord Jesus to teach you the principles of authentic Christian discipleship and mentoring. He is waiting to be your helper, teacher, and guide. I believe that He wants every one of us to exemplify His character.

Paul A. Cedar, D.Min./DD
Chairman
Mission America Coalition

Physical Characteristics of a Godly Life

INTRODUCTION

Be Conformed to the Image of His Son

This is the second book in a three-volume series about developing certain godly characteristics that others will want to emulate. It is about being, not doing. We are to become mentors. A mentor is a person whose behavior others observe and then decide, consciously or unconsciously, to emulate. Our desire is to develop godly characteristics so that Christ's life will be reflected through us.

The challenge we want to give every person that goes through this mentor training is that you will, in turn, find twelve others in your lifetime that you will mentor. Remember that mentoring is more about who you are than about what you do. You can mentor your people as a group or one at a time. If you want to do something significant with your life you should help twelve others become Christlike in their lives. During Jesus's three-year ministry on earth He gave His personal time to twelve men, who in turn, turned the world upside down. Have your people get their own books. Use your personal copy of this three-volume series that you have gone through and share your experiences with them. There is also a Mentor's Guide available for each volume. Our website at www.christianmentorsnetwork.org.

What we do is a direct result of what we are. What we are is determined by our values. Our values determine our character, and our character determines our behavior. Ask yourself these questions: "Do the characteristics reflected in my life exemplify the world's values or those of Christ?" "When people spend time with me, do they go away desiring fame, wealth, material possessions, glamour, sexual pleasure or popularity, just to mention a few, or do they desire to be more like Christ?" in other words, "What values do they desire as a result of observing my character?"

Volume 2 is about developing four personal characteristics: being physically pure, being love motivated, being of extreme value in Christ, and being Christ-actualized. These characteristics are based on the premise that God has a purpose for each believer. That purpose is explained in the eighth chapter of Romans, verses 28 and 29: *"For those who are called according to his purpose. For those whom he foreknew he also predestined to be conformed to the image of his Son, in order that he might be the firstborn among many brothers."*

God foreknew, in other words, He knew in advance, from the beginning of time, who would accept Christ as Savior. Therefore, He had predestined or purposed what they should become. His purpose is that they should be "conformed to the image of His Son." The word "conformed" means to be molded. The word "image" means likeness. God's purpose is that each believer be molded into the likeness of Christ. We are to become Christlike. Our life is to exemplify the character of our Lord and Savior Jesus Christ. When people observe us in everyday life, they should see Christ.

Only through studying God's Word, prayer, and the Holy Spirit's power can this be accomplished. We must come to an understanding of who we are in Christ. We must also experience the benefits of trusting and obeying Christ in everything. When this happens, we will have the joy and peace that the Bible promises. When we interact with other people, the loving character of Christ will be very apparent.

Having a godly life centers on being, not just doing or saying. Now, let's examine the *Personal Characteristics of a Godly Life*. I pray that this study will mean as much to you as it has to me. My desire is to be so much like Christ that others can *"Be imitators of me, as I am of Christ"* (1 Corinthians 11:1).

Roy L. Comstock, Th.D.
Chairman and Founder
Christian Mentors Network, Inc.

Physical Characteristics of a Godly Life

CHARACTERISTIC ONE

BEING PHYSICALLY PURE

I BELONG TO GOD AND HONOR HIM
WITH EVERY PART OF MY BODY

Chapter One   GLORIFY GOD WITH ALL OF YOUR
                   BODY

Physical Characteristics of a Godly Life

CHAPTER ONE

GLORIFY GOD WITH ALL OF YOUR BODY

"Or do you not know that your body is a temple of the Holy Spirit within you whom you have from God? You are not your own." (I Corinthians 6:19)

The first Personal Characteristic, being physically pure, has to do with how we honor God with our bodies. In order to bring glory to Christ, we need to control our bodies by putting them under the authority of the Holy Spirit. So now let's examine how the body displays the values of the spirit and soul: Our values and character are developed deep within our soul and those definitive traits are manifested through the body by our behavior. And, when the body is under the influencing power of the Holy Spirit it becomes an obedient servant to God's will.

Before our spiritual birth, our soul was dedicated to satisfying our body (flesh). But after receiving Christ, our life focus changes, and our soul becomes aware of its need to glorify God in our spirit. That event highlights the struggle between our flesh and spirit. The Bible tells us to keep our spirit, soul, and body blameless until Christ returns. *"Now may the God of peace himself sanctify you completely and may your whole spirit and soul and body be kept blameless at the coming of our Lord Jesus Christ"* (I Thessalonians 5:23).

Just as a husband expects his wife to be faithful to him in marriage, we are to use our bodies to the glory of God. Since it was God who made us for His own glory, He has every right to expect us to keep our body pure and blameless. King David recognized that it was God who wonderfully made him.

God has made me entirely pure and devoted to Him

"For you formed my inward parts; you knitted me together in my mother's womb. I praise you, for I am fearfully and wonderfully made. Wonderful are your works; my soul knows it very well. My frame was not hidden from you, when I was being made in secret, intricately woven in the depths of the earth. Your eyes saw my unformed substance; in your book were written, every one of them, the days that were formed for me, when as yet there was none of them" (Psalm 139:13–16).

God created man and woman in His image and likeness. Therefore, it is important to God that we represent all that God is. We can only do that by allowing God to control us and live His life in us. We must start by recognizing that God made us for His purpose, not for some purpose that we may dream up for ourselves. This is one of the reasons Christians do not believe that the transgender lifestyle is a biblical concept.

If we believe that God formed us and knitted us together in our mother's womb, then He must have intended for us to be whatever gender He created in us. If we were born with male parts God intended us to be male. If we were born with female parts, He must have intended us to be female. God does not make mistakes.

SEXUAL PLEASURE WAS CREATED BY GOD

God has wonderfully made our bodies because it pleased Him to do so. God gave man and woman the wonderful gift of pleasure because He wanted them to enjoy physical and sexual intimacy. He made one stipulation in receiving this gift, however: this marvelous experience is to take place exclusively within the marriage bed.

> *"The husband should give to his wife her conjugal rights, and likewise the wife to her husband. For the wife does not have authority over her own body, but the husband does. Likewise, the husband does not have authority over his own body, but the wife does. Do not deprive one another, except perhaps by agreement for a limited time, that you may devote yourselves to prayer; but then come together again, so that Satan may not tempt you because of your lack of self-control."*
> (I Corinthians 7:3-5).

This verse doesn't say anything about sex being sinful. In fact, it says that not to come together could cause temptation to sin.

Neither does it say that sex is only for the purpose of reproduction. In marriage, we are to come together for intimate physical, sexual, as well as emotional satisfaction. It says that if we don't do this, we could be tempted to sin. God gave us a natural sex drive and instructions on how they are to be satisfied exclusively through marriage. The Bible is very clear that anyone who engages sexually with another outside of marriage is committing the sin of fornication. And if you think about it, it's being unfaithful to their future mate.

When a spouse is sexually active with another other than their marriage partner, it is called *adultery*. The Bible states numerous times that adultery is sin. God created sexual pleasure in bounds of marriage—Satan perverted it with fornication and adultery.

> *"Let marriage be held in honor (esteemed worthy, precious, of great price, and especially dear) in all things. And thus, let the marriage bed be undefiled (kept undishonored); for God will judge and punish the unchaste [all guilty of sexual vice] and adulterous"* (Hebrews 13:4, AMP).

Jesus raised the bar on what adultery is when He said, *"You have heard that it was said, you shall not commit adultery. But I say to you that everyone who so much as looks at a woman with evil desire (lust) for her has already committed adultery."* (Matthew 5:28, AMP).

Most of us would be greatly offended if someone accused us of committing adultery. In reality, many do it every day by lusting for someone they see at work or on the street, in a movie/video, Internet, magazine, or porn shop, etc.

So, when you have solo sex while thinking of another person you are committing adultery. If you bring mental pictures of individuals into bed with your spouse in order to keep yourself aroused, you are committing adultery and defiling the marriage bed. The Bible is saying that physical purity allows our spouse to be our only source of sexual arousal. Anything else is adultery.

MAN DISREGARDS GOD'S INTENDED PURPOSE FOR THE BODY

When man is in bondage to Satan, he (or she) becomes obsessed with the desire to satisfy the flesh. In doing so, he disregards God's intended purpose for the body and seeks every possible means to satisfy the hunger of his flesh. Pleasure becomes man's passion and lust becomes his drive. All we need to do is get on the Internet to see how mankind has become self-obsessed. The drug epidemic alone is an example to what extent we will go to satisfy the unnatural demands of the flesh. Sex and violence are ingredients for Hollywood and media moguls to make millions from movies and news; while sex is the driving force behind advertising.

Satan knows how to pervert the pleasures of this world and to trap people by his deception. Once a person gets hooked on the evils in this world, it becomes very hard for them to give them up. James tells us that for a person to get caught up in the pleasures of this evil world, is to make themselves an enemy of God, *"You adulterous people! Do you not know that friendship with the world is enmity with God? Therefore, whoever wishes to be a friend of the world makes himself an enemy of God"* (James 4:4).

DON'T LIVE THE WAY THE UNSAVED DO

For the most part, the unsaved couldn't care less of what God thinks of them, because the majority doesn't act like He even exists. Many live only to please themselves and do what is right in their own eyes. Their god is the world of secular materialism and they worship at the altar of degradation. Paul tells us that, as Christians, we should be very careful not to follow their example.

"Now this I say and testify in the Lord, that you must no longer walk as the Gentiles do, in the futility of their minds. They are darkened in their understanding, alienated from the life of God because of the ignorance that is in them, due to their hardness of heart. They have become callous and have given themselves up to sensuality, greedy to practice every kind of impurity"
(Ephesians 4:17–19).

CHRISTIANS CAN BECOME OBSESSED WITH THE WORLD

When those unsaved become obsessed with the things of the world it gives Satan every opportunity to keep them from surrendering to Christ. But Christians can also become obsessed with the pleasures of this world also, because our flesh has the same desire that the world has. We have to be very careful not to feed our minds with the desires of the flesh. We need to guard our minds and our children by steering clear of violence, satanic, and heavily sexual content on TV and in movies, not to mention blocking access to Internet pornography. This increases our desire for improper sexual activity.

I did a survey of over a thousand men. Ninety-one percent of these men attend church at least one time each week and have been believers for twenty-one years. My findings showed that 46 percent of these men used the Internet for a source of pornography regularly. It also revealed that an equal percentage of these men claimed to be hooked on pornography. And remember these are men in our church.

I have a Christian friend (I'll call him Andrew) who is an architect and general contractor. While working alone on a project at a large home in Beverly Hills one day he discovered a videotape library of pornography. Andrew's curiosity got the best of him and since no one was around; he decided to watch just one video. Shocked by the explicit sexuality he quickly turned off the tape with a feeling of disgust and left the building, but the heavy sexual images stayed in his mind. Instead of surrendering his thoughts to the obedience of Christ, he allowed them to repeat over and over until the desire to see them again grew stronger and stronger. Finally, he decided to go back just one more time. Because of his position, he had a key to the house so he could come and go as often as he pleased.

He did this several times until he couldn't even drive through that part of town without being drawn to that house to see more. He said that it seemed as if his car just went there automatically as he became obsessed with sexual thoughts. Eventually, Andrew's relationship with God and his wife became very strained and his guilt caused him to separate from his Christian friends. It seemed he couldn't help himself anymore! One day, Andrew was convicted that what he was doing was ruining his life, so he called out to God, "Save me from this sin that has such a grip on me. I can't let go of it with my own power."

He fell to his knees and confessed his sin to God. He had tears streaming down his face as he repented and asked the Holy Spirit to take control of the evil desires that had gotten such a hold on him. He bound Satan in the name of Jesus and told the spirit of lust and adultery to get out and stay out in the name of Jesus. He knew that he was forgiven the moment that he confessed his sin to God.

Because the mind does not easily forget the experiences that we have, Andrew, from time to time would find those mental sexual images returning to tempt him. He realized that the best way to have continued victory was to constantly memorize and meditate on God's Word and to get into an accountability group that would pray daily for his continued deliverance. God has given him complete victory over this fleshly battle. Today, Andrew helps other men get victory over sin by sharing his story and praying for them. He is a wonderful man of God and someone that you would never imagine ever had a struggle with sexual sin. God heals completely when we give Him the opportunity.

THE UNSAVED TURN AWAY FROM GOD'S NATURAL PLAN

When people become dependent on their own wisdom and understanding, they often use it to pervert their surroundings. The degree to which they sink into sin is unbelievable.

> "Therefore, God gave them up in the lusts of their hearts to impurity, to the dishonoring of their bodies among themselves, because they exchanged the truth about God for a lie and worshiped and served the creature rather than the Creator, who is blessed forever! Amen.

For this reason, God gave them up to dishonorable passions. For their women exchanged natural relations for those that are contrary to nature; and the men likewise gave up natural relations with women and were consumed with passion for one another, men committing shameless acts with men and receiving in themselves the due penalty for their error" (Romans 1:24-27).

When we go against God's natural intention for the way that we use our bodies, it is sin. God's purpose and natural plan is for husband and wife to enjoy the sexual relationship that He has given solely to them. The Scriptures do not condone sexual activity outside of marriage. In the passage above, God's Word makes it very clear that homosexuality is sin and as a Christian, we cannot accept homosexuality as a part of God's intended plan for our life. God loves sinners, but He hates all sin and will not bless sex between persons of the same gender. As Christians, we cannot condone homosexuality. But we must love the homosexual just as we are to love all men for Christ's sake. If you are involved in a sinful sex relationship and you claim to be a Christian, you must stop immediately. Confess this activity as sin.

I do not let sin control my body any longer. I do not give into its sinful desires

God loves you and He will forgive and cleanse you of this act of unrighteousness.

When you yield to Satan's control, you will naturally love to do evil things that are just the opposite of what God wants you to do. If you have not received Christ as your personal Savior, I plead with you to do so now. When you receive Jesus Christ as your Savior, you must also yield yourself to Him as Lord. Let Him take control of your body. He will give you the Holy Spirit to help you overcome the sinful life that you've left behind.

> *"Let not sin therefore reign in your mortal body, to make you obey its passions. Do not present your members to sin as instruments for unrighteousness but present yourselves to God as those who have been brought from death to life, and your members to God as instruments for righteousness"*
> (Romans 6:12-13).

Yielding your body to the Holy Spirit is the only way to assure God's control over it. We do not have to live under sin's control. God has provided a way of escape.

God's Word has shown me how to escape temptation's power

> *"No temptation has overtaken you that is not common to man. God is faithful, and he will not let you be tempted beyond your ability, but with the temptation he will also provide the way of escape, that you may be able to endure it"*
> (1 Corinthians 10:13).

Remember that temptation always starts with our thoughts. We must learn how to get victory over temptation while it is still just a thought and not yet an action. Obedience to God's Word is God's provision for our way to escape temptation.

We can have absolute victory over temptation every time if we follow five Scriptural steps:

1. Identify: Identify the sin behind the temptation. For example, the temptation is to look at a person of the opposite sex with lust. The sin behind it is adultery. (Matthew 5:28)
2. Acknowledge: Acknowledge or confess the thought as potential sin so that God can forgive you and cleanse you from all of its unrighteousness even before you act on it. (I John 1:9)
3. Obedience: Obey God's Word. Bring the thought captive to the obedience of Christ. (II Corinthians 10:5)
4. Authority: Take authority in the name of Jesus over all of Satan and his demons' power and tell them to get out in the name of Jesus. (Luke 10:19)
5. Replace: Replace the temptation thoughts with the Word of God. Find a related Scripture and write it into a WordPower statement. You will discover how to do this in coming chapters. (Romans 12:2)

YOUR BODY IS THE TEMPLE OF THE HOLY SPIRIT

"I appeal to you therefore, brothers, by the mercies of God, to present your bodies as a living sacrifice, holy and acceptable to God, which is your spiritual worship."
(Romans 12:1).

"Flee from sexual immorality. Every other sin a person commits is outside the body, but the sexually immoral person sins against his own body. Or do you not know that your body is a temple of the Holy Spirit within you, whom you have from God? You are not your own, for you were bought with a price. So, glorify God in your body." (I Corinthians 6:18-20)

I present my body a living sacrifice, acceptable to God, which is my reasonable service

We must recognize that when Jesus Christ died for us on the cross, He not only purchased our eternal salvation, but He also bought us, including our bodies. It is only reasonable that we completely present our bodies back to Him. We must refuse to use our bodies for anything that would displease our Lord. Because we recognize His ownership, we will always see to it that we are only doing those things with our bodies that we know will bring Him honor and glory. Completely yield your body to the Holy Spirit.

I PRAY THAT YOU MIGHT ENJOY GOOD HEALTH

The health of our bodies should be very important to us for it is very important to God. God looked at everything he had made and said, *"Behold, it is very good"* (Genesis 1:31). This statement was made just after God created Adam and Eve.

30

God intends for man's body to be whole and sound; in other words, healthy.

The Random House Dictionary defines health as follows:

1. The general condition of the body or mind with reference to soundness and vigor
2. Soundness of body or mind; from disease or ailment

John said, *"Beloved, I pray that all may go well with you and that you may be in good health, as it goes well with your soul"* (III John 2).

King Solomon, in his advice to his son about the importance of wisdom, understanding, and reverence of the Lord said, *"Be not wise in your own eyes, fear the LORD, and turn away from evil. It will be healing to your flesh and refreshment to your bones"* (Proverbs 3:7-8). *"Let them not escape from your sight; keep them within your heart. For they are life to those who find them and healing to all their flesh"* (Proverbs 4:21-22)

GOOD HEALTH HAS A LOT TO DO WITH GOOD HABITS

We all have habits. Some of our habits are good and some are bad. The American Heritage Dictionary defines habit as follows:

1. A constant, often unconscious, inclination to perform some act; acquired through its frequent repetition

2. An established trend of the mind or character

3. A customary manner or practice

4. An addiction

Many of us have developed habits that are harmful to our bodies. By the frequent repetition of doing the same thing over and over, we have become addicted to, or dependent on them. Because the Bible doesn't always make it clear that a certain thing is absolutely wrong, we may rationalize that it's okay as long as we aren't hurting anyone else. One of the bad habits I had that God is giving me victory over, was overeating, as well as eating the wrong things. I have always known that being obese, even overweight, is harmful to my health, especially since there are a number of members of my family who have died of diabetes.

First, I had to come to the realization that my former eating habits were harmful to my health. Second, I had to decide that I wanted to do something about my habit. You cannot change a habit until you realize that it is wrong for you to continue doing it. At that point, you have to make a commitment to yourself to stop. Until you make up your mind to stop for your own personal reasons, you will have difficulty sticking with your decision. It doesn't matter what your habits are. They could be smoking, drinking, drugs, sexual misconduct, lying, stealing, overeating, etc. God has provided a way for you to claim victory over them.

I refuse to do anything that might get such a grip on me that I can't easily stop when I want to.

SOME OF THESE THINGS AREN'T GOOD FOR ME

We have been liberated in Jesus Christ. And because of this some Christians use this as an excuse to continue doing whatever they feel is not explicitly stated as being wrong in the Bible.

> *"All things are lawful for me,' but not all things are helpful. 'All things are lawful for me,' but I will not be dominated by anything. 'Food is meant for the stomach and the stomach for food'—and God will destroy both one and the other. The body is not meant for sexual immorality, but for the Lord, and the Lord for the body"*
> I Corinthians 6:12-13).

How do you know that something is wrong if the Bible doesn't mention it by name as being wrong? The Holy Spirit's job is to convict you of sin. If you have something in your life as a Christian that doesn't belong, the Holy Spirit will convict you of it. You will begin questioning the things in your life that seem wrong to you and the Holy Spirit will make you uncomfortable about certain things you are doing. Pay attention to what the Holy Spirit is speaking to your spirit. There is the old saying, "If in doubt, don't." The Bible says that if something seems right to you and you don't do it, it is sin. (James 4:17) When the Holy Spirit convicts you that something is right or wrong, obey Him and give that area of your life over to the Holy Spirit's control.

YOU CAN DEAL WITH YOUR BAD HABITS

Anything that we do that is against the will of God is sin. Therefore, bad habits can be dealt with the same way you deal with sin.

1. *Confess your sin to God.* He will forgive you and cleanse you from all unrighteousness, no matter how small of a thing it might be. Sometimes we forget that the small sins in our lives will become big sins if not dealt with while they are still small. Even a small bad habit needs to be dealt with.

2. *Accept God's forgiveness.* Then forgive yourself. God has forgiven and forgotten your bad habit instantly. Now you need to put the bad habit behind you so that Satan can't use it to defeat you any longer.

3. *Submit to God; resist Satan in the name of Jesus.* Bring your heart contritely before God and tell Satan in the name of Jesus to get out of your life. Remember that Jesus gave us His authority over all the power of the enemy. Also remember that the demons know who Jesus is and they must obey what we say in His name.

4. *Make a WordPower statement.* State that you know your bad habit is forgiven and that God remembers it no more against you. Speak out loud words of praise to God for His wonderful deliverance. (You will learn more about *WordPower* in Personal Characteristics Three and Four).

5. *Don't let Satan deceive you.* Don't let Satan come back and convince you that nothing happened. When

you use Jesus's name, Satan and his demons must obey; they leave. However, Satan won't give up without a struggle. He will try to convince you that you are weak or unworthy and that he is powerful. That's a lie. Jesus defeated him at Calvary. Satan has no power. Jesus gave you His authority over all the power of Satan. Submit to God and resist Satan with God's Word. Satan will leave you alone. He cannot stand against your faith.

6. *Get someone else to agree with you in prayer.* Find someone else strong in the Lord and ask them to agree with you that your victory is complete. Acknowledge together that Jesus has given you victory over Satan and your bad habit is broken. Remember that the bad habit, or sin, that you just eliminated was developed by repetition. Replace it with the repetition of your WordPower statement based on God's Word. Repeat it over and over until it becomes a permanent part of your thinking. Get into accountability with others. Remember that iron sharpens iron.

7. *Accept your victory in Christ.* "*No, in all these things we are more than conquerors through him who loved us*" (Romans 8:37).

DEVELOP GOOD HABITS TO REPLACE BAD HABITS

It is important for us to replace our bad habits with good ones. Since overeating and eating the wrong things was one of my weaknesses, I will use myself as an example. There are at least two good habits I had to adopt in order to lose the unwanted weight that I had gained.

First, I had to select a proper diet, not just give up eating sweets and starches. I had to replace the foods that were bad for me with foods that were healthy, and I also had to reduce the amount of food I was taking in. I made decisions as to how much weight I wanted to lose, and when I reached that level, how to maintain it.

Second, I selected an exercise program that was right for me to burn off the unwanted calories. My selection of a program wasn't over strenuous or too tiring, it was designed to lose weight but not strength. In fact, you will find that a good exercise program has a rejuvenating effect on your whole body. Whatever exercise program you choose for yourself, the important thing is to stick with it and have patience. Repeat it until it becomes a habit. Positive results don't usually happen overnight. Make a commitment to yourself that once you begin, you are going to continue that until you have achieved the results you want. Remember not to get discouraged. The little successes along the way will encourage you to strive that much harder for the bigger ones. It is best to make exercise a lifetime habit.

Whatever habit you are replacing, make sure you replace it with something that is beneficial to your overall health. You can have a healthy body free from immorality, drugs, alcohol, smoking, overeating, etc. But you must decide to commit yourself wholeheartedly to your objective. Ask the Holy Spirit to take control of your body.

Remember that your body is the temple of the Holy Spirit and you are taking care of your body for God's glory. A healthy body is a reflection of God's divine health in you. A healthy body helps you feel good about yourself.

My body is the temple of the Holy Spirit which is in me. I am not my own.

When you're healthy, you have more confidence in yourself. You will be more willing to try new things and attempt greater accomplishments with your life.

The first personal characteristic, being physically pure, shows us that to accomplish this we must dedicate our bodies to God's glory. We have the responsibility and opportunity to exemplify Christ through our bodies. We can say to ourselves; I daily surrender my body to the Holy Spirit's *I belong to God and I honor Him with every part of my body.* control. I am physically pure. My victory is complete in Christ.

Chapter One

GLORIFY GOD WITH ALL OF YOUR BODY

Questions for home study and group discussion

How does a person make themselves an enemy of God?
James 4:4

How has the world turned away from God's natural plan?
Romans 1:24–29

Why are Christians not to live the way the world does?
Ephesians 4:17–19

How are you to present your bodies to the Lord?
I Thessalonians 5:23, Romans 12:1

How do you know that God wants you to have good
health?   Proverbs 3:7–8, 4:21-22; III John 1:2

Notes from My Mentor's Personal Experiences

_____
_____
_____
_____
_____
_____
_____
_____
_____
_____
_____
_____
_____
_____
_____
_____
_____
_____
_____
_____
_____
_____
_____
_____
_____
_____

Scripture Memory Chapter One

"Or do you not know that your body is a temple of the Holy Spirit within you, whom you have from God? You are not your own." (I Corinthians 6:19)

Physical Characteristics of a Godly Life

CHARACTERISTIC TWO

BEING LOVE MOTIVATED

I LOVE MY FAMILY
MORE THAN I LOVE MYSELF

Physical Characteristics of a Godly Life

CHAPTER TWO

THE SAME KINE OF LOVE

"However, let each one of you love his wife as himself,
and let the wife see that she respects her husband."
(Ephesians 5:33)

The second personal characteristic of a godly life, being love motivated, has to do with the family. In no other place is it more important to remember that our purpose as Christians is to conform to the image of Christ. To have a godly life we need to make love our motive, in all relationships, especially relationships within our family. Love needs to be the golden thread that holds our families together. Whether you are married or single, this characteristic applies to you. How do you exemplify God's love in your marriages? How do you exemplify His love in parent and child relationships? And, being single, how do you exemplify God's love to your family?

My love is patient and kind. According to blueletterbible.com the word "love" is used 362 times in the NKJV Bible. For a word that is used that many times, I think it's important for us to really understand what love is and how God wants us to love.

GOD IS THE SOURCE OF LOVE

In order to have this quality of love we must get to know God in a more personal way because God is the source of all love. I John chapter 4 tells us about God's love and it shows us that when we know God then it is natural for us to love others. In fact, if we don't love others our love for God is in doubt. Therefore "others" should especially include your spouse.

> *Beloved, let us love one another, for love is from God, and whoever loves has been born of God and knows God. Anyone who does not love does not know God, because God is love. In this the love of God was made manifest among us, that God sent his only Son into the world, so that we might live through him. In this is love, not that we have loved God but that he loved us and sent his Son to be the propitiation for our sins. Beloved, if God so loved us, we also ought to love one another. No one has ever seen God; if we love one another, God abides in us and his love is perfected in us.*

> *We have come to know and to believe the love that God has for us. God is love, and whoever abides in love abides in God, and God abides in him. By this is love perfected with us, so*

that we may have confidence for the day of judgment, because as he is so also are we in this world. There is no fear in love, but perfect love casts out fear. For fear has to do with punishment, and whoever fears has not been perfected in love. We love because he first loved us. (I John 4:7-12, 16-19)

The predominant word is "love." We need to examine the word love, to see if we can understand it more clearly. The Bible says:

1. Let love be your aim (motive) (I Corinthians 14:1)
2. God is love (I John 4:8)
3. For God so loved (John 3:16)

My love is loyal no matter what the cost | Throughout his fifty-five years of marriage and fifty years of ministry, my dear friend and mentor Pastor Dr. Tex Rutledge shared the following definition of love taken from author Leo Busenglia:

LOVE – A QUESTION OF DEFINATION

"Love is trusting. Experience seems to convince us that only a fool trust that only a fool believes and accepts all things. If this is true, then love is most foolish for, if it is not founded on trust, belief, and acceptance, it's not love. Erich Fromm has said, "Love means to commit oneself without guarantee, to give oneself completely in the hope that our love will produce love in the loved person."

The perfect love would be one that gives all and expects nothing. It is only when love demands that it brings on pain. This statement sounds very basic and simple, but in practice it is difficult indeed. There are few of us so strong, so totally permissive, so trusting, as to give without expectation. In fact, a demonstrated reward is often the sole motivation for learning.

But love isn't like that. It's only love when given without expectation. For instance, you can't insist that someone you love will respond in like manner. Even the thought is comical. Yet, unconsciously, it's the manner in which most people live. If you love truly then you have no choice but to believe, trust, accept, and hope that your love will be returned. But there can never be any assurance, never any guarantee. If you wait to love only until you are certain of receiving equal love in return, you may wait forever. Indeed, if you love with any expectation at all, you will surely be disappointed eventually, for it's not likely that most people can meet all of your needs even if their love for you is great. One loves because he wills it, because it gives him joy, because he knows that growth and discovery of oneself depend upon it.

To expect something from another because it's our right is to court unhappiness. Others can and will only give what they are able, not what you desire they give. When you cease placing conditions on your love, you have taken a giant step toward learning to love (Leo Busenglia, published by Balentine Books, copyright 1972).

My love stands its ground in defending the one loved.

Everyone reading these words about love will receive a revelation of truth because God did not wait for mankind to return His love back to us. In fact, the history of Israel bears testimony demonstrating God's love continually given to a nation with no guarantee of love in return.

In I Corinthians, we read: *"Love is patient and kind; love does not envy or boast; it is not arrogant or rude. It does not insist on its own way; it is not irritable or resentful; it does not rejoice at wrongdoing, but rejoices with the truth. Love bears all things, believes all things, hopes all things, endures all things"* (I Corinthians 13:4-7).

My love always believes in the one I love.

It takes total surrender to the Holy Spirit to truly love our spouses the way that God intends for us to do. Our responsibility is to follow God's command to love one another; and as we practice love for our husband/wife in the way the preceding verse explains eventually our spouse responds in like manner. Additionally, I know from experience that as I express love to Sarah, she consistently returns love back to me in the measure with which I truly give it. This is especially true when I give my love without expectation of her returning it.

THE DO'S AND DON'TS OF LOVE ACCORDING TO THE LIVING BIBLE

Let's first look at some of the things that love does:

1. Love is patient and kind
2. Love hardly even notices when others wrong it
3. Love rejoices when truth wins out
4. Love is loyal no matter what the cost
5. Love always believes in the one loved
6. Love always expects (hopes for) the best
7. Love stands its ground in defending the one loved

Now let's look at some of the things that love does not do:

1. Love is not haughty (proud or vain)
2. Love is not selfish
3. Love is not rude
4. Love does not demand its own way
5. Love is not irritable or touchy
6. Love does not hold grudges
7. Love is never glad about injustice

If you applied each of these do's and don'ts of love to your marriage, what do you think the results would be?

Although for the next couple of chapters we will be focusing on the husband and wife relationship, I would like to challenge our singles to pay particular attention as well! Because the concepts and examples we can learn about men and women not only benefits us in marriage but in every day life. Make sure to use this section to gain insight in better handling relationships with those of the opposite sex in our lives right now and for those

My love always expects (hopes for) the best

who might one day become part of our lives while we encounter one another in our workplaces, within our families, and engage in various social interactions. If you are currently unmarried, there is a possibility that someday you might be. Use this time to pray for your future "other." Pray they too are learning these same concepts and hold these same values dear as you do. Then when you do meet, coming together as one will be as seamless as possible.

THE HUSBAND AND WIFE RELATIONSHIP

Let's start with the husband and wife relationship. Today, more than ever, there is a great need for marriages to reflect Christ's perfect love to a lost and corrupt world. We desperately need Christlike marriages functioning in stark contrast to the world's standard of love which is predominated with selfishness, lust, and pride. A key passage of Scripture that tells what the relationship between husband and wife should be is found in Ephesians chapter 5.

> *Submitting to one another out of reverence for Christ. Wives submit to your own husbands, as to the Lord. For the husband*

is the head of the wife even as Christ is the head of the church, his body, and is himself its Savior. Now as the church submits to Christ, so also wives should submit in everything to their husbands.

Husbands, love your wives, as Christ loved the church and gave himself up for her, that he might sanctify her, having cleansed her by the washing of water with the word, so that he might present the church to himself in splendor, without spot or wrinkle or any such thing, that she might be holy and without blemish. In the same way husbands should love their wives as their own bodies. He who loves his wife loves himself. For no one ever hated his own flesh, but nourishes and cherishes it, just as Christ does the church, because we are members of his body. "Therefore, a man shall leave his father and mother and hold fast to his wife, and the two shall become one flesh." This mystery is profound, and I am saying that it refers to Christ and the church. However, let each one of you love his wife as himself, and let the wife see that she respects her husband." (Ephesians 5:21-33)

There is another important thing to point out in these verses. Notice that Paul talks to the husbands and wives separately. Men and women see, feel, and show love in completely different ways. So much so that it is practically impossible to discuss them together.

Let's take a look at them individually.

HUSBAND'S PERSPECTIVE

Let's look at the role of the husbands. Many of the men I know, have read these verses with blinders on. They gravitate to the verses that appeal to the male ego like where it says, "Wives must submit to your husband's leadership." As men especially agree with that word "submit" and are quick to point out that the dictionary defines it as follows:
(All American Heritage Dictionary)

1. To yield or surrender oneself to the will or authority of another; to give in.
2. To allow oneself to be subject to; to acquiesce.

Men also like it where it says, "For the husband is head of the wife," as well as the statement, "So you wives must willingly submit to your husbands in everything." Men get excited here to find three biblical directives for the wife:

1. She must submit
2. He is in charge
3. She must submit to him in everything

Unfortunately, some men misconstrue this meaning and think, "Wow! Since God has put her in her place; she has to do what I say because the husband is supreme ruler of his domain. My wife must give me what I want when I want it or she will disobey God.

My love hardly even notices when others wrong it.

Further, God must be a man because He set up the lines of authority this way. So, here's proof that women are the weaker sex, lorded over by her master and ruler, her husband."

Gentlemen, if you are one of the men who think this way, I have news for you. By pulling out this section of Biblical "text" while ignoring its original framework, in effect we have thwarted its full insight.

Wait until you understand what this really means! It's time to quiet down and take a closer look at God's Word because as husbands, we will be held accountable before God for our actions in this matter. We may do well to look at the Scripture that we quoted from Ephesians 5:21, "*Submitting to one another out of reverence for Christ.*"

Remember what the dictionary said? "Surrender oneself, give in or acquiesce." In this respect, husband and wife are equal. Both are to honor Christ by giving in to the other. This means that we are to submit, give in, and acquiesce to her. That sounds a little more like equality than servitude. Our equality is in Christ. Jesus said that God is no respecter of persons.

In looking at the last part of verse 22, we see that the wife is to submit to her husband in the same way she submits to Christ. In verse 23 it says that the husband is to be in charge in the same way that Christ is in charge of His body the Church (and remember that He gave His very life to take care of it, because He loved the Church more than He loved Himself). And in verse 24, it says that your wife is to submit to you as the Church summit to Christ.

It seems, that husbands being in charge; and wives submitting has some conditions:

1.   In the same way she submits to Christ

2.   As Christ is in charge of His body the Church
3.   Just as the Church submits to Christ

HUSBANDS ARE TO LOVE THEIR WIVES

My love rejoices when truth wins out.

Verse 25 gives us the key to understanding these conditions. *"Husbands, love your wives, as Christ loved the church and gave himself up for her."*

The Word of God compares the relationship between husband and wife to that of Christ and His body the Church. Men, we need to be transformed through prayer and the Word to become Men of God in our daily lives, as well as faithful husbands who love our wives more than we love ourselves. Too many times we copy the behavior of the world failing to honor our wives' role within the family; elevating our own position by putting her down through our words and actions. But the Bible tells us not to conform to the world's way of doing things. *"Do not be conformed to this world, but be transformed by the renewal of your mind, that by testing you may discern what is the will of God, what is good and acceptable and perfect"* (Romans 1:2). The world's motive is selfishness.

Love is the result of God's presence in our lives. Since God indwells us through the Holy Spirit, then it only makes good sense that as we let the Holy Spirit take control of our thoughts, we will then develop the inner values resulting from God's love. Adopting God's values of love will change our attitudes about love and eventually our actions will manifest His love.

John 3:16 tells us that God so loved that He gave. True love is motivated by giving rather than by taking.

Many men solely focus on their wife's role as taking care of their own needs instead of putting their wife's needs before their own. Christ gave up all His glory in heaven in order to serve our needs on earth demonstrating He loved us more than He loved Himself.

Men, we have to give up our pride, selfishness, and our desire to be served so that we can truly see life from our wife's viewpoint. We must treat her with mutual respect by setting aside our selfish pride and honor her as an equal partner in the marriage relationship. Men, our wives are not there just to please our every desire. Loving our wives more than ourselves means sacrificing our personal desires while carefully anticipating what she needs and wants—especially when it is different from what we want; then doing it.

WIFE'S ROLE OF SUBMISSION

Just as men have one role within the marriage, to love their wives as Christ loves the Church, our wives have just one role as well. The wife's role is to submit to their husbands just as the Church submits to Christ. While on the surface, it might seem to a man that women have it pretty easy compared to the man's role of sacrificing himself for his wife; let's think about things from her point of view. She's instructed to submit to her husband. Are we as husband's worthy of submission? Are we walking in the Word and submitting ourselves to the Holy Spirit's control to ensure that we are making the right decisions for our family? Can you imagine how frightening it would be for your wife while trying to be godly by submitting to you, her husband but you are not walking with the Lord nor surrendering your will to the Holy Spirit? What confidence does she have that you are making the right decisions for your family when you are relying on yourself?

We must be very careful in our roles as "leaders of the home." 1 Peter 3:7 warns us to stay mindful so our prayers will not be hindered. *"Likewise, husbands, live with your wives in an understanding way, showing honor to the woman as the weaker vessel, since they are heirs with you of the grace of life, so that your prayers may not be hindered."* This is how much importance God puts on the husband/wife relationship that if a husband allows his relationship with his wife to slip, his prayers will be affected. Consequently, as husbands we have be very aware of how we use our authority over our wife. If we take advantage of her submissiveness, our own spiritual life will suffer.

WIVES PERSPECTIVE

Like husbands, wives also have one role in marriage - to submit. Unfortunately, in our culture submission is viewed as a degrading concept meant to keep women silent and "in their place." But in God's word, this cannot be further from the truth. This is yet another "Truth" that Satan has perverted with this deception by destroying the Biblical foundation of marriage consequently pulling the rug from under our feet. Today it's common knowledge that our divorce rate has soured to over 50 percent—even within the Christian community! So, I ask, "How's that working for you?" Personally, I think it should be more than raising the eyebrows of our spiritual leaders and forcing them to look at why it has become this way. I believe as long as the biblical teaching of submission and husband's leadership within the home remain taboo, especially within the church, the very biblical foundation that sets the order for a successful marriage is forfeited. In our culture, everyone seems to be doing it on their own and relying on their own strength instead of the principles found in the Bible and the power of the Holy Spirit. That's a recipe for failure.

SUBMISSION IS THE ULTIMATE ACT OF LOVE

Submission is not the Lord's intention of making wives feel inferior to their husbands. Christ shows us how a Christian household is to remain in balance. Without this balance, chaos ensues. Husbands submit to Christ, wives submit to their husbands; together the husband and wife, like the Church, submits to Christ together; everything in balance and in order. If any part of this equation is off it will affect your entire life. Biblical submission does not mean marital slavery. If that is how your husband makes you feel, he needs to go back and reread the previous section written for husbands. Christ calls for wives to be submissive to keep the household balance and also to show love to their husbands in a way he can understand. For the most part, men understand respect and honor, but at times need some help in the "showing love department."

Now women, on the other hand, understand love but sometimes require help with respect and honor. What I'm trying to convey is that this is not a means to "hold women back" or "put them in their place," but rather as an insight as to how to love your husbands in a way he can comprehend; just as the Bible calls Him to love you in a way that you understand.

Ephesians 5:22 says *"Wives, submit to your own husband, as to the Lord."* Ironically, the Bible calls for wives to submit to their husbands many times, but rarely does it call for wives to love their husbands. Have you tried submitting without love? It cannot be done, at least without long-term side effects such as bitterness or resentment. How can wives possibly be expected to "yield or surrender oneself to the will or authority" of their husbands without love? You can't. God, our perfect counselor, knows women well enough to know that "loving" is not their biggest problem. They are emotional beings but needed to be told how to put their love into an action that men can understand and feel the sense of love from; just as husbands needed to be told to love their wives in a way that they would understand. Wives can accomplish putting their love into a form that their husbands can feel through the action of submission and respect.

The Bible has given us everything we need for a healthy marriage, but it means going completely against our flesh and what the world says we should do. Therefore, in order to have a healthy marriage, its foundation must be on the transforming power of the Holy Spirit. We must die to ourselves daily and put what's best for our spouse before our own desires. Whether that means to love or submit.

Just as Ephesians 5:22 tells husbands to love their wives, verse 33 tells wives to see to it that she deeply respects her husband. If you ask men, which they would rather have, love or respect, they will answer respect the majority of the time. Just as wives do not think they need to earn their husbands' love, husbands do not think that they need to earn her respect. Husbands need to love their wives with unconditional "agape" love without expectation. Likewise, wives need to demonstrate that same unrestricted love to their husbands, by loving them without conditions or expectations graciously respecting them even when they don't deserve it. In this way, the wife is fulfilling the command to deeply respect her husband. We will talk more about this in the next chapter.

As we discover what it means to love and respect our spouse the way God has called us, we'll be compelled to love our spouse more than we love ourselves. If we claim to love Christ, we need to check our attitude about love. But if we are treating our spouse the way the world treats their spouse then it only serves to prove that God's love is not in us. So, I urge you to be transformed in your mind by the power of His Word and surrender your heart to the Holy Spirit you may learn to grow in your love for your spouse with an unconditional love that only comes from God.

How will we know God is doing a work in our hearts regarding love? As we begin to experience the fruit of His gracious love flowing through us to our spouses; our love becomes more patient and kind. We lose the need to act out of pride or jealousy. Our previous desire to dishonor our husband/wife or act out of selfishness or be quick-tempered subsides. In God's love toward our partner, we have no need to keep a record of their offenses. We won't delight in "I told you so" but will rejoice with living in truth. We will be protective of them; trust and invest in them with hope, because this type of love never fails us.

Chapter Two

THE SAME KIND OF LOVE

Questions for home study and group discussion

How can we show the same kind of love to our spouse that Christ showed the Church?   Ephesians 5:25–27

What should our motive be in the marriage relationship?   I Corinthians 14:1

What is God's attitude concerning love?
I John 4:8, John 3:16

Name seven things love does.
I Corinthians 13:4–7

Name seven things love does not do.
I Corinthians 13:4–7

Physical Characteristics of a Godly Life

Notes from My Mentor's Experiences

_____

_____

_____

_____

_____

_____

_____

_____

_____

_____

_____

_____

_____

_____

_____

_____

_____

_____

_____

_____

_____

_____

_____

_____

_____

Scripture Memory Chapter Two

"However, let each one of you love his wife as himself, and let the wife see that she respects her husband." (Ephesians 5:33)

CHAPTER THREE

MAKE LOVE YOUR MOTIVE

"And hope does not put us to shame, because God's love has been poured into our hearts through the Holy Spirit who has been given to us." (Romans 5:5)

As I mentioned in the previous chapter, love is the immersion of God's presence in our lives. Through grace, God indwells in us through the Holy Spirit, so it only makes good sense that as we yield to His loving Spirit, He begins a transformation of our inner values and to govern our thoughts. Adopting God's values of love will change our attitudes about love, and eventually our actions will manifest that love.

In Galatians, we read that the Holy Spirit will produce the fruit of love in us. *"But the fruit of the Spirit is love, joy, peace, patience, kindness, goodness, faithfulness, gentleness, self-control; against such things there is no law"* (Galatians 5:22-23).

(On page 1,102 of The Open Bible references, you will find the following comments concerning the attributes of love:)

The fruit of the Spirit is love. Living in love is the only way we can fulfill the will of God in our lives. The believer must become love-inspired, love-mastered, and love-driven. Without the fruit of the Spirit, love, we are just making noise. *"If I speak in the tongues of men and of angels, but have not love, I am a noisy gong or a clanging cymbal"* (I Corinthians 13:1) The fruit of the Spirit is love and it is manifested in joy, peace, long-suffering, goodness, faith, meekness, and temperance. Therefore, the attributes of love are:

1. Joy is love's strength
2. Peace is love's security
3. Long-suffering is love's patience
4. Gentleness is love's conduct
5. Goodness is love's character
6. Faith is love's confidence
7. Meekness is love's humility
8. Self-control is love's victory

> *"And hope does not put us to shame, because God's love has been poured into our hearts through the Holy Spirit who has been given to us."* (Romans 5:5)

HUSBANDS SHOULD LOVE THEIR WIVES

My love is not haughty (proud or vain)

Remember what Ephesians 5:28–30 says, *"In the same way husbands should love their wives as their own bodies. He who loves his wife loves himself. For no one ever hated his own flesh, but nourishes and cherishes it, just as Christ does the church, because we are members of his body."*

To sum it up, husbands have one major responsibility and privilege to love their wives as Christ loves His Church. Men, we need to be less concerned about what our wives are "doing" for us and more focused in prayer for who she is "becoming" in Christ. In addition, let's stay humble before God to insure we love her the way God loves us. *"However, let each one of you love his wife as himself, and let the wife see that she respects her husband"* (Ephesians 5:33).

Husbands, as you lead by doing your part in loving your wife more than you love yourself before long, you may discover that your wife will be increasingly happy in doing her part. Respect, submission, praise, and honor are progressive responses to real love. If you continue to love your wife as Christ loves the Church, she will eventually manifest that same spirit of love and respect in return. Be obedient to God's Word and don't give up! But keep this in mind: it's really not a matter of you "doing", it's a matter of you "becoming" who God has called you to be as a husband.

So, don't be demanding and selfish but learn to be perfect (mature) in your love for your wife. If you insist on your own way all the time, she'll grow weary of your demanding behavior and resist you. She needs to know that you truly love her and that you are interested in satisfying her needs. We have to create an atmosphere of trust for our wives because if she gives into you; she's got to be confident that you will never take advantage of her and end up feeling used. We need to learn to love perfectly. We can only do that in Christ.

> *"There is no fear in love, but perfect love casts out fear. For fear has to do with punishment, and whoever fears has not been perfected in love. We love because he first loved us"* (I John 4:18-19).

Remember, we love God because He first loved us. Christ gave Himself on Calvary before we even knew about it. Once we found out what He had done for us, we accepted His love and returned our love to Him by accepting His gift of eternal life. As our love for God grows, our love automatically grows for our spouse. Plan to spend time every day with your heavenly Father. *God is love.* The more time we spend with Him the more we will become like Him.

WIVES SHOULD RESPECT THEIR HUSBANDS

Ladies, I hope you were listening closely to what I was telling the men, because almost everything I told them applies to you as well. The reason I spoke so directly to the men is because when I first wrote and taught these principles it was to a group of fellow inmates at the California State Prison. This group of men needed to hear how they should treat their wives, perhaps even more than the men who attend your church. Many of these inmates had forgotten, if they ever knew, how to love. I prayed that somehow, I could share some principles that would help them and their families when they were released to go back to their homes. I believe that discovering God's love is their only hope for staying out of prison and becoming productive men in their communities.

God's Word explains that wives have very clearly defined responsibilities to their husbands. We have already talked about most of them.

Husbands are not the exclusive object of God's command to love: *"And so train the young women to love their husbands and children"* (Titus 2:4).

Wives, the same can be said to you about your relationship to your husband. Husbands *My love is not selfish.* respond to a wife who is not afraid to express her love for him. As you may know, often just expressing love verbally is not enough, though he does need to hear it from you. And, how many times have you longed for him to back up his words of love with his actions? Because actions speak so loud you can't always hear what a person is saying. Wives demonstrate to your husbands love through the act of biblical submission and respect.

LOVE AND RESPECT

Love and respect are two of the most important attributes in any healthy relationship, but unfortunately, they are too often withheld when marital misunderstandings or offenses bring in worldly thinking. But in Ephesians 5:33 we will find our foundation for healthy relationships. *"However, let each one of you love his wife as himself, and let the wife see that she respects her husband"* (Ephesians 5:33).

The Bible clearly states that husbands are to love their wives, while the wives are to respect their husbands. Why the two different directives? Because; men and women are infinitely different. Typically, men can respect easily, but often struggle expressing love. While women, on the other hand, usually have no problem showing love but set an expectation their husband that he earns her respect before it's given. And, here is a big reason why today's marriages are failing by the masses! This one, critical and foundational biblical concept of love and respect is being overlooked and under taught.

HUSBANDS WITH LOVE AND RESPECT

It seems God has given men the innate ability to respect. For example, gentlemen, let's say your father had been abusive toward you: while you can still respect the position, he holds in the family. Whether you love him, or even like him, is an entirely different matter. So, the respect you give to someone they might deserve because of the position they hold, may be completely different than your feelings about them personally. Men, this attribute can be profitable in the workplace or between you and male friends, but when it comes to your wife, it can be a hindrance because she does not always require your respect; she requires your love.

Most women do not feel loved from being respected. And, while your wife still wants your respect, she needs, deserves and craves your love. She desires to know that you love her. She feels loved when you tell her you love her, and when you demonstrate affection without a constant expectation to move into the bedroom. Show her you love her by listening to her heart as well as her words. Anticipate her "honey do list" before she asks you! Make it a "honey done" by asking her "babe, what do you need?" Demonstrate your attention to her needs by helping her with the kids, being the first to the car to help her put away groceries or cleaning up after dinner. Being attentive to her feelings and truly caring about what she is thinking, and feeling is how your wife can feel your love.

WIVES WITH LOVE AND RESPECT

While men have an incredible ability to respect; women have that same capacity for expressing love.

By contrast, in using the same example above; if a father is abusive toward his daughter, her respect for him quickly disappears even though she may still love him. When someone is unkind a woman may still find it in her heart to love them but due to our old nature, any previous respect is now gone. In a woman's eyes, respect must be earned. It is not passed out freely to everyone. For her, it takes time developing respect for someone and unfortunately it can be lost in a moment. And when it is lost, it takes that much more to get that respect back.

Here's what wives need to understand about their husbands: your husband feels loved by your respect shown for him. If your words demonstrate you do not believe in him, don't trust him, minimize his achievements, or make light of his masculinity; divorce is not far behind. Men feel loved from being honored and revered. They need to feel needed, like the protector and provider of the family. When our actions or attitudes say that we don't need them or our lives could go on without their provision, they do not feel loved.

THE CIRCLE OF LOVE AND RESPECT

What do we find when we put these two elements together? Men feel love through respect and women feel love through attentiveness. But ironically, sometimes the very things that make others feel loved are the very things that we are poor at displaying. We are reminded that in Luke 9:23 calling us to deny ourselves daily. As we conform to the image of Christ that may often involve stretching beyond our "comfort zone" we are uncomfortable with or not used to.

Husbands, if we asked your wife if you respected her, she'd probably confidently answer that you do.

On the other hand, if one of her close girlfriends asked if you loved her; would that be a whole different story? Now, if someone asked your wife if she loved you, she'd very likely reply that she does. But if she was asked if she respected you by a close girlfriend—I think you get the point... The truth is that our love and respect should both be given unconditionally. Neither should be earned nor should they ever be used against each other.

When a husband allows his wife to become a lesser priority, his love for her diminishes in her eyes and her respect for him quickly follow suit in the wrong direction! Now, wives, don't think that because I started with the husbands that you are not also fully responsible for starting this negative downward spiral by allowing disrespectful words to come out of your mouth! Once this cycle begins, it becomes a very slippery slope; especially when you don't even realize the true root of the problem.

James 4:1-3 (NIV) says: *"What causes fights and quarrels among you? Don't they come from your desires that battle within you? You desire but do not have, so you kill. You covet but you cannot get what you want, so you quarrel and fight. You do not have because you do not ask God. When you ask, you do not receive, because you ask with wrong motives, that you may spend what you get on your pleasures."*

The bottom line is that both love and respect are born out of our yielding to God's heart first. When we see our God larger than our misunderstanding with our spouse, we can learn to rise above our "old nature" and live in the "new man" an exercise the grace Christ modeled by giving His life for us. Love and respect are what keeps the good days good. Let me challenge you with this that if your marriage is "less than good" these days try changing your thinking. Bring the love and respect back into your relationship! You might be thinking how will this work?

He's not reading this book and he doesn't know to change his thinking! Here's the beautiful thing: when you allow the Holy Spirit to transform your thinking first, then start loving and respecting your "other" again, they will once again become "your better half." You must first allow God to change you.

YOUR SPOUSE DOESN'T ALWAYS DESERVE YOUR LOVE AND RESPECT

Here's the hard part, I know that your spouse doesn't always deserve your love or your respect. God knows that I don't always deserve Sarah's respect. But aren't you glad that God doesn't love us according to how much we deserve it. That is what grace means, "unmerited favor," giving favor where and when it is not deserved. God commands wives to respect their husbands. It would certainly be a lot easier for you if your spouse loved you according to what the Bible says. But if they don't already love you that way, then at best, it will take some time before they do. I also challenge you to concentrate on the commands God has given you in the Scriptures and let the Holy Spirit do His work on the inside of your spouse. Remember that love is the fruit of the Spirit.

It is very important that both of you spend time daily in God's Word. Let the Holy Spirit govern your lives in grace. Pray together and ask God to teach you how to love and respect each other in His perfect love.

PLEASE DON'T BE STUBBORN

I know that many of you have a great deal of bitterness and resentment toward your mate for the wrongs that he or she has committed within the marriage.

Don't be stubborn. Let God's love melt away that hardness and replace it with His tender mercies. Remember Love hardly ever notices when others wrong it.

My first wife and I separated after twenty-one years of marriage because I was bitter and hurt. I was too stubborn to realize that it was me wanting my own way that was driving the wedge between us. I spent time thinking about all the things I thought I was being cheated out of. My selfishness is what caused us to finally separate and never get back together again. As a Christian leader, this was the most devastating experience of my life. It was more devastating than losing my business, millions of dollars, and then serving a four-year sentence in the California State Prison system.

Through God's grace, I got my life back into fellowship with my Lord and He forgave me of all my selfish sinfulness and restored me to Himself. I was privileged, through God's love and forgiveness, to marry Sarah. I am now concentrating on proving my love to Sarah. Because, by nature, I am such a selfish person, I find that I must spend time every day with the Word of God learning to understand and apply God's principle of unconditional love. I have not mastered it, but when I do practice it, I can tell what a difference it makes in my ability to love Sarah more than I love myself.

I have discovered that as important as it is to tell Sarah that I love her, that is not enough. My actions must express how very much I love her. It is easy because she is concentrating on loving me and proving her love for me by obeying God's Word and respecting me even though I don't deserve it. My responsibility in our relationship is not to inspect her fruit to see if the Holy Spirit is producing love in her life.

My responsibility is to walk in the Spirit and let Him completely control me, so that God's love will automatically manifest itself through me.

The late Dr. Tex Rutledge taught us about how to apply God's grace and love to our marriage by learning to be gracious toward our spouse. Following is a guideline that he used when counseling premarried, as well as married couples to help them understand the importance of graciousness in marriage. The author of the material is unknown.

My love is not rude

GRACIOUSNESS: THE LIFE BREATH OF MARRIAGE

The word "gracious," means accepting, kind, courteous, pleasing, and merciful. Grace may be defined very simply as "unmerited favor." That is, it is kindness shown regardless of whether it is properly earned or deserved. It is the father welcoming home the prodigal son who has squandered his father's wealth. It is Jesus welcoming the woman who was a sinner, or saying to the hated tax collector, *"Zachaeus, make haste and come down, for I must stay at your house today"* (Luke 19:5). It is Stephen praying for those who stoned him saying; *"Lord, do not hold this sin against them"* (Acts 7:60). It is that quality in the heart of God that causes Him not to deal with us according to our sins, or to requite us according to our iniquities. (Psalm 103:10) In fact, it is what love always must be when it meets the unlovely, the weak, or the inadequate.

If that is what God's grace is, what is it in marriage? How is grace demonstrated in the day-to-day living out of marriage? Grace is demonstrated when you are:

1. A Becomer rather than a Reformer
2. An Encourager rather than a Critic
3. A Forgiver rather than a Collector

A Becomer rather than a Reformer

First, a "Becomer" helps others become all that it is possible for them to become. This word is similar to the words "enable" or "enabling." The "Becomer" makes things easier or possible. Too often a person discovers that marriage, instead of freeing him or her to become all that he or she can be, is stifling and limiting. This may occur because the spouse adopts the role of a Reformer. A Reformer tries to get their spouse to meet their standards. An insecure person wants their mate's behavior, beliefs, and attitudes to be just like their own—and he is threatened by any real or supposed differences. Some people seem to have an almost-irresistible urge to reform or improve their partners, in some respect.

Sometimes even the tiniest habits seem to require corrective action: the way one dresses, the way one walks or the way one squeezes a tube of toothpaste. I am not, of course, suggesting that we have no need to change and to grow in hundreds of ways. The problem comes when the husband or wife appoints himself or herself a "Committee of One" to see that the necessary change is enacted, and in doing so says, in effect, "You must change. I can't really accept you as you are until you get busy and do it." The result is that Grace is smothered and all genuine desire for love-motivated change is quenched.

Paul urged the believers in Ephesus to be, *"Completely humble and gentle; be patient, bearing with one another in love."* (Ephesians 4:2, NIV) Another translation says, *"Making allowances because you love one another"* (Amplified). That's an important concept. If you love your spouse, you can accept the fact that they will do things differently and will think differently than you. Paul Fairchild put it this way, "Differentness is another way of saying, 'individuality'"

I trust you have taken time to consider the positive qualities and unique traits that you and your spouse possess.

Be thankful to God for each other's uniqueness! You should praise and thank each other for each of your particular qualities.

It is not your responsibility to take on the job of Reformer in your relationship with each other. Your task is to learn to trust God to do the work and to provide an atmosphere of acceptance that allows Him freedom to work. God accepts you as you are, and this acceptance frees you to develop and grow. If you can learn to accept each other "as you are" it frees each of you to grow.

This does not mean that you may never talk about definite faults and detrimental character defects. You can—and you must—talk about them in an honest manner. But leave the responsibility for change to the other person and the Grace of God.

Differentness adds excitement and interest to a relationship. The marriage itself will reflect more strength and interest because of the combination of two individual personalities. "Sameness" can be dull.

An Encourager rather than a Critic

The second demonstration of grace is encouragement instead of criticism. To encourage means to help the other person to have courage. You believe in the other person. It is saying, "You can do it, I am behind you and confident in you." It is

My love does not demand its own way.

building up rather than tearing down. It is giving positive suggestions rather than negative criticism. It is being concerned about changing yourself rather than the other person.

Since criticizing and suggesting changes only increases resistance, consciously or unconsciously, and since prodding and pushing only increases the problem by decreasing understanding, love, and acceptance between you, discard it. Determine to give the most wholehearted love and acceptance possible - without conditions. Instead of accepting with spoken or unspoken reservations, genuinely accept each other as you promise today. Vows are nothing if they do not become a way of life—a daily commitment of life. Your vows are not to educate, reform, and restructure your mate, but to love. The crucial commitment of marriage is the pledge to be the right mate to the other person.

Are you committed to being the right mate here and now? Do that, be that, and you will make a change for the better for the both of you. Where criticism is a commodity and forgiveness is in short supply, you have a ready market for marital disaster.

A Forgiver rather than a Collector

Finally, grace is demonstrated by being a Forgiver rather than a Collector. This implies a willingness to relinquish hurts and to restore a relationship after you have been offended. Proverbs 17:9 says, *"LOVE forgets mistakes; nagging about them parts the best of friends."* Maturity in marriage means, being able to forgive and forget. To a Christian, this power is the very core of your experience. You have been loved, accepted, and forgiven by God—and this is your greatest gift. Because of it you can face the future fearlessly with joy and gladness and without undue anxiety; you can also forgive others. Not that such action is easy from a human standpoint, but it was not easy for God either—it cost Him His Son on the cross.

Forgiveness is hard. It is especially difficult in a marriage when troubles come, when fears of rejection and humiliation surface, and when suspicion and distrust arise. Forgiveness hurts, especially when it must be extended to a husband or wife who doesn't deserve it, who hasn't earned it, and who may misuse it. It hurts to forgive.

My love is not irritable or touchy Forgiveness costs—especially in marriage when it means accepting instead of demanding repayment for the wrong done; where it means releasing the other instead of exacting revenge; when it means reaching out in love instead of relishing resentments. It costs to forgive.

Forgiveness does not demand guarantees. Less than true forgiveness is offered whenever a husband or wife says to the other, "I'll forgive you if you promise never to do that again." That is conditional forgiveness—a deal! But the forgiveness of which the New Testament speaks is never equated with driving a bargain. Christian forgiveness risks the future; it gives all and it risks all. Forgiveness does not recall—you forget grievances, you do not collect them.

Will you experience the joy of forgiveness and restoration with each other? Will you readily go to the other one and confess sin and ask forgiveness?

The path of forgiveness leads to the expression of Grace and the building of intimacy. Remember, these and other demonstrations of Grace can ensure for your marriage the maxim: "and they lived happily ever after."

THE DELICATE SUBJECT OF SEX

Next, I'd like to briefly discuss the delicate subject of sex. Often, we're told that money is the number one cause of divorce. I'm not sure I agree. Speaking from the husband's perspective, it is more likely to involve a couple's sexual intimacy. Countless couples build up more resentment and deep-rooted bitterness in this area than in any other. One partner often feels rejected, while the other may feel used.

Following is a Scripture that explains God's attitude about the physical relationship between husband and wife.

"But because of the temptation to sexual immorality, each man should have his own wife and each woman her own husband. The husband should give to his wife her conjugal rights, and likewise the wife to her husband. For the wife does not have authority over her own body, but the husband does. Likewise, the husband does not have authority over his own body, but the wife does. Do not deprive one another, except perhaps by agreement for a limited time, that you may devote yourselves to prayer; but then come together again, so that Satan may not tempt you because of your lack of self-control"
(I Corinthians 7:2-5).

Both husband and wife are equal in the bedroom

When it comes to making love, it is clear by the above Scripture that husband and wife are equal, having full right to a loving response from the other. So actively communicate your desires to each other and talk over how you're feeling about sex. Don't let silence between the two of you about this delicate topic lead to awkwardness and eventually bitterness; especially if you're experiencing inhibition expressing your feelings. Instead, take responsibility for learning the desires of your mate enhancing your intimacy. If you don't you may be partly responsible for causing them to sin.

If you have physical or emotional problems that keep you from enjoying this pleasurable, God-given relationship with your spouse, seek professional support. Ask your pastor to recommend a Christian physician or godly counselor that can help you in this area of your life.

SERVING OTHERS IS THE BEST WAY TO PROVE YOUR LOVE

My love does not hold grudges

Serving others is a true demonstration of love. Everyone likes to feel important and one of the best ways to make another person feel important is by serving them. Most men I know have the idea that their wives are supposed to serve them, fix their meals, clean the house, and take care of the children. Without saying it, we expect our wives to serve our every need! Not only is that the wrong attitude, but it may serve to further antagonize a spouse when both work outside the home. Men, if we want to be the leader in our home, we need to follow Jesus's example.

Jesus teaches us if we desire to be leaders we must first learn how to serve. In Matthew 20:26–28, He says, *"It shall not be so among you. But whoever would be great among you must be your servant, and whoever would be first among you must be your slave, even as the Son of Man came not to be served but to serve, and to give his life as a ransom for many."* So, don't assume the role of "king of your castle" demanding your family to cater to you! Our role as father and husband is to exhibit leadership by serving our wives and children first.

My pastor calls this "servant leadership." And, he makes it very clear that if someone isn't willing to serve others in the congregation, they will not be asked to serve in a leadership position within our church. With that in mind, maybe couples in premarriage counseling should be strongly cautioned that if they are more interested in serving their own needs above their future spouse first; they should remain single!

A number of years ago, during the Promise Keepers movement, men were challenged to go home and try to outserve their wives. I went home all fired up and determined I was going to express my love to Sarah by outserving her. Wow, did I soon have a revelation! Sarah was vastly more experienced in serving than I was. I failed miserably.

My love is never glad about injustice

During that time, I kept asking myself, "How can I out-serve Sarah?" Finally, I realized that I didn't have a chance so I had just better concentrate on serving her as best I could.

From that experience through the years I have developed a little guide to remind me of what I need to do. I call it the Do-Go-Sow principle.

DO

This part of the principle is based on what most of us know as the "Golden Rule." Jesus said, *"So whatever you wish that others would do to you, do also to them, for this is the Law and the Prophets"* (Matt. 7:12). In other words, treat your spouse the way you would want them to treat you, as if your position was reversed. So, I asked myself, "If I were Sarah how would I want to be treated?" Then I try to treat her that way.

GO

We have all heard the saying, "Going the extra mile." *"And if anyone forces you to go one mile, go with him two miles"* (Matt. 5:41). That means to practice doing more than is required. There are things around the house that I may think are Sarah's responsibilities, but I do them anyway. Guys, housekeeping, washing dishes, vacuuming floors, and changing baby's diapers may not be in what you think of as your traditional roll, but it could help your wife more than you realize! And that's especially true when both spouse's work outside the home.

SOW

You reap what you sow. *"Do not be deceived: God is not mocked, for whatever one sows, that will he also reap"* (Galatians 6:7) According to this verse, we receive according to the measure with which we give.

"What comes around goes around" as the ole saying goes. Love your spouse by anticipating her needs at every opportunity. Why measure what you are willing to give by what you think you'll get back? With that kind of thinking this principle works against you. Instead, consistently seek ways to serve first and, in time, all your needs will be taken care of. Luke 6:38, says *"Give, and it will be given to you. Good measure, pressed down, shaken together, running over, will be put into your lap. For with the measure you use it will be measured back to you."* This verse makes plain that as we give (serve) we receive more will more back than what we invested. Serving Sarah is the greatest way I have found to prove my love for her, and her love has been returned back to me more than I imagined!

Chapter Three

MAKE LOVE YOUR MOTIVE

Questions for home study and group discussion

What are the attributes of love?   Galatians 5:22–23

What does the Bible say about wives respecting the husband?   Ephesians 5:33

How can I show my love and respect for my spouse in our intimate relationship?   I Corinthians 7:2–5

What is the key to men becoming the leader in our homes? Matthew 20:26–28

How can we out serve our spouse using the Do-Go-Sow principle? Matthew 5:41, 7:12; Galatians 6:7–9

Physical Characteristics of a Godly Life

Notes from My Mentor's Personal Experiences

_____
_____
_____
_____
_____
_____
_____
_____
_____
_____
_____
_____
_____
_____
_____
_____
_____
_____
_____
_____
_____
_____
_____

Scripture Memory Chapter Three

"And hope does not put us to shame, because God's love has been poured into our hearts through the Holy Spirit who has been given to us." (Romans 5:5)

CHAPTER FOUR

TRAIN UP A CHILD GOD'S WAY

"Train up a child in the way he should go;
even when he is old, he will not depart from
it." (Proverbs 22:6)

I have talked a lot about love in this approach to the family. Love is the only hope families have in this world today. As we learn how to love from God's Word through the Holy Spirit working in our lives, the most important priority in our family is to make love our motive in everything. This is particularly true in relationships with parents and their children.

If you don't have children, please don't slide past this chapter. Each of us either have children, know people who do, or still have parents themselves and are therefore still a child to someone. So no matter your current situation these words still apply to you. Let's constantly be open to what the Lord is teaching us and, most importantly, remember to be prepared at all times to minister to those the Holy Spirit will be bringing into our lives.

An important place to practice godly characteristics is right your own home with your children. I urge you to study each characteristic and make it a part of your life so that you will exemplify God's character to your children. The opportunity to mentor your own children is no doubt one of the greatest responsibilities a parent has. Our children do what they see us do so this is one place that you cannot say, "Do as I say, not as I do." Whether you exemplify good or bad behavior does not make a difference because statistics indicate that children grow up to be like their parents in a very high percentage of the cases. Generally, when children become different than their parents it is because they found someone else that they gain greater respect for and whose character they emulate. Parents, if you study these mentoring characteristics just that you can exemplify Christ's love to your children, that's more than enough reason!

We will start by examining Ephesians 6:1–4: "*Children, obey your parents in the Lord, for this is right. "Honor your father and mother" (this is the first commandment with a promise), that it may go well with you and that you may live long in the land. Fathers, do not provoke your children to anger, but bring them up in the discipline and instruction of the Lord."*

TRAIN UP A CHILD IN THE WAY HE SHOULD GO

As parents, we are responsible to train our children in the ways of the Lord. They are to learn from us how to conform to the image of Christ, by loving God with all their heart, mind, and soul, and loving others more than they love themselves. Children will also

I am bringing my children up with the loving discipline and instruction of the Lord

learn from us how to manage their own lives while depending on the Holy Spirit for guidance. As parents, we must learn how to walk in the Spirit in order to teach them how to resist Satan's attacks in their lives–if not from us, who will teach them?

It's essential to train our children to develop absolute values based on God's Word. That's the only hope of survival in this world today. Children look to us as role models and will likely handle circumstances in their lives in the way they observe us handle ours. Our children's thinking is often a reflection of our thinking and their actions often become a reflection of ours. To some degree, when we look at our children, we are looking into a mirror at ourselves. That's why it is so important we exemplify the characteristics of Christ in our own lives.

Obviously, the sooner we can engrain these godly characteristics in our children the better. So, if your children are young, praise the Lord, you can start today! Your kids will grow up witnessing your example and truly benefiting from it.

If your children are older, there may need to be some redirection depending on their age and understanding. Have a talk with them about your past parenting and their past behaviors as well as the reason behind your change of heart. You might have to be willing to offer them an apology for any inappropriate examples set for them in the past. I would encourage you to: share with them how Christ has opened your eyes, changed your heart, and has convicted you to become the godly parent they deserve. Tell them your desire that things be different. And, share your heart for your family to become more Christlike and be a godly example to the world around you.

There may be resistance at first, but as you pray for the Lord to open their eyes and soften their hearts, your children will begin to experience the real changes in you and become more open. Again, the key is them seeing your example first because they won't change if they don't see a real change in you. But remember, if you have this "big talk" with them about how much God is changing you then how you expect them to change; you must go ahead of them first to set the example yourself.

CHILDREN WHO OBEY GOD'S DIRECTION RECEIVE GOD'S BLESSING

As parents, it is our responsibility to teach our children how God wants them to act toward us. Too many parents leave these important lessons to teachers and preachers. But it is not their job, it's ours as parents. Let's teach our children that God has special blessings in store for them if they obey His principles with regard to honoring parents.

As you read this section, it will help you explain to your children what God expects from them in the parent/child relationship. We cannot demand honor and respect; it must be taught, so instruct them in these principles while they are young. But if your children get these concepts while they are young, when they grow up they will not forget them.

Help them discover God's purpose for giving them the parents He did. Understand that at times, they may have felt cheated, but careful to explain that God has given them instructions on how they should act toward you. Conveying God's directions in the Scriptures that He has promised to give something to them in return.

There are two things that we are to teach our children:

1. Obey their parents
2. Honor their parents

The word "obey" is defined in the American Heritage Dictionary as:

1. To carry out or fulfill a command, order, or instruction
2. To carry out or comply with a command, order, or request

This definition does not mention anything about our feelings. God instructs parents to act on His Word, not on our emotions. We are to lovingly discipline our children according to the Bible, not by the wisdom of the world. Assure your children God doesn't require us to correct them without already knowing the outcome will be good for them. Lastly as a parent, if we must punish them for disobedience, it is imperative we display a calm demeanor and ensure that they understand we love them unconditionally as God loves us. Comfort along with instruction should immediately follow a repentant heart.

Another item God has instructed us to teach our children, is to honor. The definition of "honor" is as follows:

Wisdom gives me a long and good life.

1. Respect, esteem, and reverence
2. Homage, and expression of high regard
3. Reverence, a feeling of deep respect or devotion

4. Veneration is the feelings of respect, love, and awe, especially for one whose wisdom, dignity, sacredness, rank, or age merits such attention.

5. Deference is respect or courteous regard for one, which takes the form of yielding to his judgment or wishes.

Honor deals with our feelings as well as our obligations. Honor is something that cannot be demanded. Although the Lord tells us we are to honor our parents without exception, we must realize that true honor can only be taught by example. But if you feel as though your children do not honor or respect you right now, maybe you should ask yourself, why? Next, ask the Lord to reveal things that you may have said or done that respect might have been compromised. Becoming aware of being a parent who lovingly demonstrates respect and honor should be top priorities now. Also be willing to apologize to your children when you have made mistakes, behaved sinfully in front of them, or have acted dishonorably to them.

This might be a process that your family will have to walk through. May I suggest you convey to your family that, as a parent (or as parents) "we are working to become godly examples?" So starting today, you will give them the respect they deserve and in turn, you will be requiring their respect. If respect is not shown, there will be consequences. Bear in mind, if you fail to demonstrate to your child respect, they will not display respect for you! Again, let me emphasize you must be willing to apologize to your child first, if you did not show them their due respect. In turn, they must be taught that the consequences work both ways. When they are disrespectful to you, they must also apologize to you and; depending on the circumstances may require additional correction or subsequent punishment.

GOD HAS PROMISED YOUR CHILDREN TWO THINGS

If they obey and honor you, God has promised them the following:

1. A long life
2. A life full of blessing

A long life indicates a life free from poor health, stress, worry, and starvation. You can't have a long life if you are always sick or hungry. A life of blessing indicates that you will participate in God's promise in John 10:10, where Jesus said, *"The thief comes only to steal and kill and destroy. I came that they may have life and have it abundantly (in fullest measure)."* It comes back to us when we teach our children to be accountable in the ways of the Lord. They learn respect and the values you are trying to instill in them keeping them off a road that leads to a short life. They are more likely to abstain from a life of additions, immorality, greed, bitterness, and anger. They have had a godly foundation to make good choices which lead to a long life full of blessings. Isn't that what we all want for our children?

God promises our children He will reward their loyalty and love for us. In all things, we must remember to make love our motive. I'd urge you to read I Corinthians 13:4–7 several times and learn how to help your children apply the "do's and don'ts" of love to your relationship.

GOD WILL HONOR HIS WORD

The following Scriptures in Proverbs talk about parent and child relationships. Written almost entirely by King Solomon who was considered the wisest man who ever lived; I would urge you to meditate on these verses until their truth becomes ingrained into your thinking. Let them guide you in keeping your children

My wisdom comes from my trust and reverence

accountable to our Lord's teachings. They will also help you understand God's attitude about loving discipline. Isaiah 55:11 says *"So shall my word be that goes out from my mouth; it shall not return to me empty, but it shall accomplish that which I purpose, and shall succeed in the thing for which I sent it."* God will honor His Word.

> *"The fear of the LORD is the beginning of knowledge; fools despise wisdom and instruction. Hear, my son, your father's instruction, and forsake not your mother's teaching, for they are a graceful garland for your head and pendants for your neck"*
> (Proverbs 1:7-9).

WISDOM IS THE TREE OF LIFE

> *"My son, do not despise the LORD's discipline or be weary of his reproof, for the LORD reproves him whom he loves, as a father the son in whom he delights. Blessed is the one who finds wisdom, and the one who gets understanding, for the gain from her is*

better than gain from silver and her profit better than gold. She is more precious than jewels, and nothing you desire can compare with her. Long life is in her right hand; in her left hand are riches and honor. Her ways are ways of pleasantness, and all her paths are peace. She is a tree of life to those who lay hold of her; those who hold her fast are called blessed" (Proverbs 3:11-18).

"Hear, O sons, a father's instruction, and be attentive, that you may gain insight, for I give you good precepts; do not forsake my teaching. When I was a son with my father, tender, the only one in the sight of my mother, he taught me and said to me, "Let your heart hold fast my words; keep my commandments, and live. Get wisdom; get insight; do not forget, and do not turn way from the words of my mouth. Do not forsake her, and she will keep you; love her, and she will guard you."
(Proverbs 4:1-6)

"Prize her highly, and she will exalt you; she will honor you if you embrace her. She will place on your head a graceful garland; she will bestow on you a beautiful crown. "Hear, my son, and accept my words, that the years of your life may be many"
(Proverbs 4:7-10)

"My son, keep your father's commandment, and forsake not your mother's teaching

*Bind them on your heart always; tie them around
your neck. When you walk, they will lead you; when
you lie down, they will watch over you; and when
you awake, they will talk with you. For the
commandment is a lamp and the teaching a light,
and the reproofs of discipline are the way of life"*
(Proverbs 6:20-23).

DISCIPLINE ISN'T ENJOYABLE WHILE IT'S HAPPENING

Now that we have discussed how and why children should behave, what happens when our children are disobedient? It's our job to discipline. The Bible says, *"Train up a child in the way he should go: and when he is old, he will not depart from it"* (Proverbs 22:6) The Scriptures in the book of Hebrews talk about training a child the way God trains us. It says,

God's correction is always right and for my best good.

*"It is for discipline that you have to endure. God is
treating you as sons. For what son is there whom
his father does not discipline? If you are left without
discipline, in which all have participated, then you
are illegitimate children and not sons. Besides this,
we have had earthly fathers who disciplined us and
we respected them. Shall we not much more be
subject to the Father of spirits and live? For they
disciplined us for a short time as it seemed*

*best to them, but he disciplines us for our good, that
we may share his holiness. For the moment, all
discipline seems painful rather than pleasant, but
later it yields the peaceful fruit of righteousness to
those who have been trained by it"*
(Hebrews 12:7-11).

Although it may be unpleasant while being
administered, disciplining your children will bring good
results. The following Scriptures show those benefits:

*"Whoever spares the rod hates his son, but he
who loves him is diligent to discipline"*
(Proverbs 13:24).

*"Discipline your son, for there is hope; do not
set your heart on putting him to death"*
(Proverbs 19:18).

*"A youngster's heart is filled with rebellion,
but punishment will drive it out of him"*
(Proverbs 22:15).

*"Do not withhold discipline from a child; if
you strike him with a rod, he will not die. If
you strike him with the rod, you will save his
soul from Sheol"* (Proverbs 23:13-14)

Be careful how you interpret this passage, it does not
give you permission to beat your children, whether out of
anger or frustration. You must be loving and gentle in
your discipline so that it corrects the wrong behavior but
does not physically or emotionally harm the child.

"The rod and reproof give wisdom, but a child left to himself brings shame to his mother" (Proverbs 29:15, 17).

I know that God loves me because He is training me through His loving discipline

In Ephesians 6:4 tells parents to bring their children up with the loving discipline and instruction of the Lord. It also teaches us two things that we are not to do:

1. Don't keep on scolding them
2. Don't continue nagging them

When you do this, it brings out two reactions:

1. It makes them angry
2. It makes them resentful

Instead, we are to train them with love. This is done in two ways:

1. With loving discipline
2. With godly advice

The most important thing to remember about discipline is consistency! Discipline only works when a child knows beyond any doubt that when they are disobedient and break the rules; there will be consequences. But there is no such thing as "one size fits all" discipline so the consequences may vary from family to family.

I no longer love this world and all it used to offer me.

And the punishment needs to fit the child and the circumstance. The bottom line: there needs to be consequences for disobedience.

Parents don't make meaningless threats. If your punishment involves the threat of something being taken away or staying home instead of going someplace fun—follow through! No lessons were learned, and no behavior was changed. Therefore, your "discipline" was useless and each time this happens you lose ground. Your word will mean nothing to them because they know you won't follow through. You'll lose credibility in their eyes. Why should they listen to you or follow your rules when there are no real consequences for doing otherwise? Once you give in and allow the child to get away with their disobedience, you have lost the battle.

Children will always test the line and push it to the extreme to find it. If no boundaries are set, they will keep pushing the mark until someone finally shows it to them. Unfortunately, then, that person may be a police officer. By that time, you won't need to punish them—a judge will do it for you just before they are sent to jail; and the consequences will be far greater than you ever imagined!

As a parent, you have eighteen years to turn a child into a functioning adult, suitable for society. The only way this can be done is through consistency and discipline. Our children need to be shown a line that does not change and does not waiver. They must to know that when they break the rules there will be consequences—every time. There is a reason why parenting is called one of the hardest responsibilities that a person can ever do. It takes godly wisdom, hard work, and will power. So stand your ground!

BOTH PARENTS MUST AGREE

Having both parents in full agreement is the cornerstone of consistency in discipline. Because it's impossible to have consistency without both being on the "same page" regarding disobedience; everyone must know what will happen when the rules are broken.

Make sure "rules of the house" are established and fit into your family's lifestyle. Whenever possible, base them on Scripture. For example; having our actions exemplify the "Fruit of the Spirit" (Galatians 5:22-23), or the Ten Commandments (Exodus 20:1-17). Obviously, not all the rules can be to be tied with Scripture. Therefore, those rules could fall under Ephesians 6:1–3 *"Children, obey your parents in the Lord, for this is right. Honor your father and mother, which is the first commandment with promise: that it may be well with you and you may live long on the earth."* The point is to ensure your family walks in accordance to God's Word and under His wisdom.

Based on the age, I recommend a "family meeting" to discuss the new rules and express their feelings. Truly listen to what they have to say and if you agree with their arguments, the rules may be adapted accordingly. Discuss the possible consequences of disobedience to what both parents have agreed upon: whether that entails taking special items away for a period of time; being grounded or losing privileges. After the meeting, every family member should understand the rules. Make sure the instructions are simple and easy to understand. Print them out and put them in a visible place until they are committed to memory. Hopefully as a parent, this will also remind you that when a rule is broken, punishment must be carried out, not just threatened.

Please keep in mind, that when establishing rules and consequences, those need to fit the dynamic of your family. Most importantly, once your family' guidelines are established, follow through and enforce them! Children need to learn that consequences follow disobedience. Just make sure any punishment fits into your family plans. For example, let's say your family is visiting friends at their home. Now it's time for your child to pick up toys, put shoes on, etc. Just when everyone is ready to leave, they become resistant and then disobedient: It's not wise to say something like this... "Nathan, if you don't help put away toys right now, you are not coming back here again!" More than likely he knows that statement is not true. So he defiantly ignores you thus making you even more upset! He knows you're not following through on that threat, therefore you have no credibility. Furthermore, when you make an emotionally irrational threat of punishment, be prepared to follow through with it and suffer the consequences also! In this case, if he is "never coming back here again," next time make prior arrangements to keep Nathan home even if that means staying home yourself. Be careful of the warnings that you speak to your child. Only speak what you know you can follow through. Remember: consistency, consistency, consistency!

THE PURPOSE OF GODLY DISCIPLINE

Be on guard not to take our children's discipline personally. Instead of disciplining them with love, we punish them out of our anger. It's essential to learn the purpose for discipline. Once we understand correction from God's perspective, it is easier to be more objective about it.

The purpose of discipline is teaching our children the difference between right and wrong. But that doesn't mean according to the world's definition. As parents, we must learn God's Word well enough to understand what God says is right behavior or wrong behavior. Therefore, don't say to your children, "Do as I say, not as I do," because as parents, we lack authority in disciplining them for behavior that they have learned from us without first seeing our repentant heart.

As both parents come to know God's Word, they can come together in complete agreement. Nothing confuses children more than having their parents disagree on what is right and wrong conduct.

Above all else, make love your motive! God holds the family in high regard, and He compares the family with that of His kingdom. He calls us His children. In the Bible, Jesus is called the first of many brethren. The husband and wife relationship is used as an example of Christ's relationship to His Church, the Body of Christ.

PARENTING THE ADULT CHILD

During one of our mentor training classes, one of the guys asked, "What should be our relationship to our married children?" This is a very important question. Just because our children are grown doesn't mean they are not our children anymore, but we do have to understand how the relationship will change.

COMMUNICATION

One of the most important roles as a parent of adult children is communication. Whether you have already raised your family in a godly home or have more recently come to walk with Christ, nothing says how much you love, until you show how much you care. If you haven't already done so, develop a habit of keeping up with what's happening in your children's lives: birthdays, special events, and sometimes just to say, "I miss you." While, we as parents want to give them the negative space to build their own lives and friendships, that doesn't mean we can't be a voice of encouragement and care when they need us. Our home should always be "a home away from home" where our children enjoy the warmth of the holidays, celebrations, or just everyday occasions.

As we get older, we might experience health or other problems that may pull us more toward challenging circumstances. But I also would encourage you to be honest about what is going on in your life without dwelling on the negative. I think this is why some adult children have a hard time keeping in touch with their parents. Who wants to talk with someone, when all they do is complain? So as we age, let's remember to keep our joy in the Lord and dwell the good things in life.

Another reason why adult children may become more disconnected is the fear of ridicule about how they're living their lives. Even though you will always be their parent, remember that your time of having a say in their lives has ended. Once they leave our homes and are in charge of their own life, we now come into a new season of becoming our child's friend. No longer can we punish them for the sin in their lives. That is completely the Lord's responsibility now. We can however, be their advocate and intercessor in prayer. So if your adult child is now living a sinful life—pray. If you try to parent them, it will only hinder this new friendship that is developing.

Keeping these things in mind, you can begin to build a wonderful friendship with your child, and that is the goal at this point. You prayed them through their teenage years, now you pray them through adulthood.

SPEND TIME TOGETHER

We all know how life can get in the way—so don't let it! Make an effort to spend time together. If you do not live close to each other, this might take more of an effort. Make it a priority to plan a trip to see them. Understand that if your adult child now has a family of their own it might be more difficult for them to come see you—so you go to them. Don't fall into the trap of "guilt trips." Try to remember what it was like traveling with young children. It might be easier for you, in this time of your life, for you to go see them.

If you do live close to each other, plan time to get together. Not just for special occasions, but for fun too. Plan weekly or monthly dates and spend time together catching up on each other's lives. It will probably be these times they will look back on with the fondness of memories. Oftentimes, a truly deep friendship will come from making this effort of putting life on the back burner for a while and nurturing this relationship. The key is making the time. Again, it has to be a conscious effort on both your parts.

PRAYER

This is obviously the most important thing you can do for your child—no matter how old they are. Especially since they might be no longer consulting your opinion on things or running their "new ideas" by you; so all you can do is pray.

May I suggest, praying that their hearts will be open to hearing the Lord's voice and that they would follow His direction. If they are yet unmarried, pray for their future spouse and that the Holy Spirit would begin preparing their hearts for the time He brings them together. Pray for your grandchildren or future grandchildren. Pray that they would come to know Christ at a young age and their hearts will be pliable to the Word of God. Pray for your child as a parent; that the Lord will give them wisdom and discernment with their children. Ask them how you can be praying for them. Then follow up with them on those prayer requests. Bottom line is be diligent about praying for them!

PARENT/CHILD TO FRIENDS

Understand that this process begins when children are in high school, but the actual transformation, in your child's eyes, is practically overnight. They will more than likely come to this conclusion when they turn eighteen, graduate high school or when they leave for college. This is a hard thing for most parents, but the more you release your child to grow and trust that the Lord is in control, the deeper the mutual respect will grow with your "new friend." If you don't already have calluses on your knees from praying them through high school, you will now! You might even slip now and then forgetting that your opinion is now merely a suggestion. And, they just may remind you of that too! Allow this to be a growth experience for the both of you. It's a great time to apologize to your child for your shortcomings. Make sure you convey that you understand that they are adults now and are responsible for making their own decisions, as well as for the consequences that might follow. Lastly may I suggest, let them know that this is new for you too and ask for their patience with you during this transition.

BE ON GUARD AGAINST SATAN'S ATTACK IN THE HOME

Satan is a formidable adversary. His mission is to destroy the family. Christians need to be on guard against Satan's attack in our homes. Our enemy uses any means that he can to separate you from your commitment of daily conforming to the image of Christ. Be on guard from strife between husband and wife, children and parents, as well as brother and sister. Our advisory will do everything he can to stop the family from glorifying Christ. Satan will attack you in the same way that he tempted Jesus through:

1. The lust of the flesh
2. The lust of the eye
3. The pride of life

He will tempt us with the lust of the flesh through illicit sexual activities, drugs, alcohol, etc.

He will tempt us through the lust of the eye by making us desire every material thing that we see, thus drawing us deep into debt causing undo financial stress on the family. Continuing financial duress causes strong disparity that may eventually break families apart.

Satan will tempt us with the pride of life. This ignites selfishness and a compelling drive for what we think we deserve from life; placing our own feelings, well-being, and ourselves first. We become demanding that others acquiesce to our desires and wishes.

We stop looking at things from the other person's point of view; especially God's point of view. There's a growing compulsion to start looking outside of the home for the things we feel we are missing. Eventually, if these temptations go unchecked, Satan will deceive us to the point that accepting sin becomes an alternative, leading to adultery, divorce, drugs, and other iniquities contrary to God's Word.

GOD IS NOT ANGRY WHEN WE FAIL

It's unnecessary to get into all the situations that we may find ourselves in when we stray from the Word of God. The Apostle Paul said,

> *"Do not love the world or the things in the world. If anyone loves the world, the love of the Father is not in him. For all that is in the world—the desires of the flesh and the desires of the eyes and pride of life—is not from the Father but is from the world"*
> (1 John 2:15–16).

We all have sinned in these areas because we are alike. According to Romans 3:23, *"All have sinned."* That means that we're all in the same boat. God is not mad at us for sinning. He loves you and stands ready to forgive you! *"If we confess our sins, he is faithful and just to forgive us of our sins and to cleanse us from all unrighteousness"* (1 John 1:9).

It doesn't matter if you have lied, committed adultery, or if you are divorced, God loves you. There is no sin so great that He will not forgive you. *God is love.* He loves you just as you are. If Satan is attacking your family in any way, give it to

Jesus and ask Him to help you overcome. I would also urge you to seek your pastor's help.

Make sure that each family member understands how to receive salvation through Jesus Christ. Then teach them how to completely surrender their lives to the Holy Spirit. Use your authority in Jesus's name to command Satan to be loosened off your family. Teach your family to put on the full armor of God. And remember, to humble yourself before God and resist Satan—he will flee from you!

GO BACK TO THE BEGINNING

Christ forgave me of all my sin and cleansed me from all unrighteousness

Revisit the beginning of chapter 2, called, "The Same Kind of Love," page 36 and reread the "do's and don'ts" of love. Then practice applying them to each member of your family. God will richly bless you and heal your family. Satan is a defeated foe. You and your family are the property of God, purchased by Christ's blood at Calvary. Satan has no rights. You can tell him to get out in the name of Jesus, and he must go!

The second personal characteristic of a Godly Life, Being Love Motivated, is learning how to love your family more than you love yourself. You can only learn how to love your family by spending time with God in prayer and in His Word. God is love!

Chapter Four

TRAIN UP A CHILD GOD'S WAY

Questions for home study and group discussion

How are we to raise our children?   Ephesians 6:4

When God disciplines us, what does it prove?
Hebrews 12:5–11

What are the results of training a child according to biblical
principles?   Proverbs 22:6

When you discipline your children, what does it prove?
Proverbs 13:24

What are the results of not disciplining a child?
Proverbs 19:18, 22:15, 23:13–14, 29:15, 17

Physical Characteristics of a Godly Life

Notes from My Mentor's Personal Experiences

_____
_____
_____
_____
_____
_____
_____
_____
_____
_____
_____
_____
_____
_____
_____
_____
_____
_____
_____
_____
_____
_____

Scripture Memory Chapter Four

*"Train up a child in the way he should go;
even when he is old he will not depart from it."*
(Proverbs 22:6)

CHARACTERISTIC THREE

BEING EXTREMELY VALUED

I KNOW AND LOVE WHO I AM IN CHRIST
I AM A PERSON OF EXTREME VALUE

Chapter Five   KNOW WHO YOU ARE IN CHRIST

Chapter Six   BE TRANSFORMED BY THE
                 RENEWING OF YOUR MIND

Chapter Seven   YOU ARE OF EXTREME VALUE
                 IN CHRIST

Chapter Eight   WORDPOWER IN ACTION

Physical Characteristics of a Godly Life

CHAPTER FIVE

KNOW WHO YOU ARE IN CHRIST

"For as he thinks in his heart, so is he."
(Proverbs 23:7)

The third personal characteristic of a Godly Life, being extremely valued, has to do with the person—primarily our self-image. As others emulate our lives, it is important that we exemplify a positive attitude about who we are in Christ. In order to do that, we must first know how special we are to our Heavenly Father, because of our relationship in Christ.

We will be discussing several aspects of our lives as related to the way we see ourselves, and what we think about ourselves. How we think, see, and feel about ourselves determines how we project ourselves to others as well as how we set goals for ourselves in life.

Self-image (also referred to as ego) is a term that has to do with how we really feel about ourselves. If you believe you could never be successful at God's purpose for your destiny, then you will never even try to succeed.

Self-image is comprised of an individual's values and how they affect whom he/she truly is. The opinion you hold of yourself is shaped by the thoughts programmed by others through your experiences from childhood, marriage, friendships, church, social gatherings, relational interactions, as well as many other factors. But even then, it's usually not a true assessment of the real you. Because when you doubt you can succeed, you believe a lie about yourself! You are not successful primarily because you don't believe you can be.

YOUR SELF IMAGE DETERMINES YOUR GOALS

The reason self-image is vitally important is that it determines the kinds of goals you'll set for yourself. It also defines how you'll interact with others. And, the quality of your communication becomes especially important in husband/wife and parent/child relationships. So, when the Bible says that we are to love others as we love ourselves, but we are having trouble loving ourselves; this inability will have an adverse effect on our ability to love others. Therefore, it's difficult to (1) comprehend the love that God has for us, (2) for us to receive God's love and to express that love to others.

Our goals for serving God and our family, in addition to others, are affected by what we believe about ourselves. As we think about setting goals for our life, we may initially think big, as if there were no boundaries. But eventually all the negative emotions that have accumulated over our lifetime begin to bog down our ambitions. So now when evaluating our lofty goals in the light of all our negativity there's a tendency to lower our goals feeling that they are either unrealistic or unobtainable.

For example, what if a medical student is capable of becoming an excellent surgeon? What if his dream in the first year of college was "more than anything in the world, I want to have a career in the medical field and eventually become a surgeon"? He has all the abilities it would take, but in his own mind he just doesn't realize it. Perhaps he feels he can't accomplish this goal because all his life someone has told him, "You can't do that. You'll never amount to anything." Maybe as a kid, every time he tried to do something like go out for the swim team, get a job after school, or strive for good grades, his dad always said, "You're not good enough, you don't have what it takes." Consequently, after being told that time and time again throughout his life, he really begins to believe it. Now his past negativity begins clouding his aspiration to become a surgeon. He rationalizes his own abilities less than they truly are, or his goal unrealistic and beyond his reach. Subsequently, he allows his dream to fade away and resets his sights on working a job as an orderly at a local hospital.

Although, there *is* nothing wrong with this per say: because he is truly capable of achieving much more but has settled for significantly less than he's capable—all due to his low self-image; his full potential is missed! Using all his abilities, this goal could be reachable if he would only make the effort and believe that he could do it!

It is obvious that this student's low self-image is having a negative effect on his goals. What he thinks of himself is determining the goals that he is choosing for his entire life. And to a certain extent, the same thing is true of every one of us. In the next section, we'll be addressing how our thoughts affect our self-image and how God sees us. Once we understand how He sees us everything changes!

The self-image that each of us have of ourselves is not entirely of our own making. What we believe about our abilities and ourselves is generally what has been programmed into us for years by parents, teachers, relatives, peers, and our environment. Unfortunately, most people have a very poor image of themselves or in today's narcissistic culture; an overinflated and self-centered ego. The good news is that we don't have to be stuck for the rest of our lives with the self-image that others have programmed into us. With the guidance of the Holy Spirit, our self-image can change. And, through time, perseverance, and surrender to God's loving purpose for our life—what we think and feel about ourselves will be remade!

YOU CAN LIKE YOURSELF AND BELIEVE IN YOURSELF

As a child, I lived in fourteen foster homes and my life was filled with fear and loneliness. Everything about my childhood communicated to me that I was inferior. Moving from one foster home to another, I wondered why I couldn't have a mother and father like all the other kids. Even though my mother visited me in my foster homes, I began to hate her because I was convinced she could have taken care of me if she really wanted to. I got it into my head that she just wanted to have a good time without the responsibility of kids. Then one day my father came to visit me, but I hadn't seen him since I was a baby. I didn't even know who he was, so I didn't want to have anything to do with him either. In heart and mind, as with my mother: if he really loved me, he wouldn't have taken so long to come to me. My early family life made me feel that I wasn't worth anything to anyone. After all; if my own parents didn't want me, why would anyone else? And if no one else loved me, how could I love myself?

WHAT IS SELF IMAGE?

Self-image is not necessarily the image we have of ourselves that we portray to others. It is not what we want other people to think about us. It is what we honestly think about ourselves—deep down inside.

The Bible says, *"As a man thinks in his heart, so is he"* (Proverbs 23:7). What is in a person's heart, his thoughts and values is what he really is, and it will eventually express itself through his actions. Remember, that our *thoughts* become our values. And progressively, our *values* become our character. Then our *character* will eventually be reflected in our *behavior.*

Even though we may present a great facade to the world around us giving every outward impression of being confident and competent; but inside we are a bundle of fears and insecurities. We harbor self-doubt in our abilities to achieve success resulting in stagnation and unproductive, unfulfilled lives. Low self-esteem keeps the majority of us from striving for and reaching the pinnacle of success. People I've met in life that have a good self-image are individuals who have worked diligently to change their attitudes and abilities. This enables them to grow from within through God's Word to become successful.

If every time you're faced with a new challenge, your reaction is "I can't do it," you can be sure that your self-image is low! In contrast, a healthy self-image says, "how can I initiate a plan to get it done?" When your perception remains negative; you'll continue to give up without trying, procrastinate, and never give yourself a chance to prove your capabilities. Because when we are afraid to fail, we won't put in the necessary effort to be successful. Watch out for these signs of a low self-image:

1. Negative thinking.
2. The inability to set robust goals.
3. An "I can't do it!" attitude.
4. Fear of failure.
5. The fear of other people's opinion if you fail.

These are all inherent signs of a low self-image.

The low self-image of many Christians keeps them from having the abundant life that Jesus promised. They don't believe they deserve it, so they don't attempt to accomplish much in their lives simply because they don't believe they can.

> *"And Jesus said to him, "'If you can'! All things are possible for one who believes'"* (Mark 9:23). Jesus also said, *"Truly, I say to you, whoever says to this mountain, 'Be taken up and thrown into the sea,' and does not doubt in his heart, but believes that what he says will come to pass, it will be done for him"* (Mark 11:23). *"And to the centurion Jesus said, "Go; let it be done for you as you have believed." And the servant was healed at that very moment"* (Matthew 8:13).

Surprisingly, most of us don't really believe God and the promises He has made to us. Because our self-image tells us that we are not worthy to receive His blessings. Our self-image determines what we are willing to accomplish in our daily walk with God. When our self-image is high, and we have confidence in the promises and truths of God's Word,

I believe all things are possible for me | there is no limit to what we can accomplish in life and for His glory. So let's set high goals with the assurance of God's promises that these goals are reachable.

In Romans chapter 7, Paul describes his own personal struggle between his new nature in Christ and his old sin nature that was still pulling him away from what was right. What was true then, remains true today; we all have this same inner struggle that Paul experienced. If we don't come to grips with it, it's going to continue to affect our self-image.

PERHAPS YOU HAVE FELT LIKE PAUL

> *"For I do not understand my own actions. For I do not do what I want, but I do the very thing I hate. Now if I do what I do not want, I agree with the law, that it is good. So now it is no longer I who do it, but sin that dwells within me. For I know that nothing good dwells in me, that is, in my flesh. For I have the desire to do what is right, but not the ability to carry it out. For I do not do the good I want, but the evil I do not want is what I keep on doing. Now if I do what I do not want, it is no longer I who do it, but sin that dwells within me.*
>
> *So I find it to be a law that when I want to do right, evil lies close at hand. For I delight in the law of God, in my inner being, but I*

*see in my members another law waging war
against the law of my mind and making me
captive to the law of sin that dwells in my
members. Wretched man that I am! Who will
deliver me from this body of death? Thanks be
to God through Jesus Christ our Lord! So then,
I myself serve the law of God with my mind,
but with my flesh I serve the law of sin."*
(Romans 7:15-25)

The Scriptures above attest that even Paul, who was the writer of a great deal of the New Testament, had the same struggles that we face. He was torn between his desire to please God and the pull from his old fleshly nature that *I desire to do God's perfect will all the time* craved to do wrong. Even though our past sins have been forgiven by God's divine grace, many still haven't let those offenses go and left their failure behind. And way too often, we tend to hold to our mistakes reminding us of just how weak we really are. Consequently, this "wrong thinking" serves only to disqualify ourselves from God's unconditional love. When this negativity prevails, Satan uses it to make us feel guilty and inadequate.

Programmed by our past, we begin to believe things about ourselves that keep us stuck in one place. So even when we desire to act in God's purpose, we fail because in our minds we've failed before! The voice in our head says, "Don't you remember what happened the last time you tried to do what God wanted you to do? So why try again? You'll only fail." Our mind has difficulty letting go of painful memories. So I'm encouraging you hold on to God's Word! Believe and accept God's forgiveness then put the past where it belongs—in the past!

Make that choice today and break the chains of self-doubt and begin enjoying the abundant life that God has planned for you!

THIS INNER STRUGGLE IS NORMAL

Paul's life serves as a stark reminder this inner struggle isn't solely experienced by new Christians. Previous to Romans, Paul had also written Corinthians, making the following statement: *"Imitate me, just as I also imitate Christ"* (I Corinthians 11:1). Then Paul went on to say that others should imitate him. But he also went on to admit this inner struggle even after telling others to follow his example! That confirms it's normal for us to have this turmoil between our old nature and our "new." So it's not a matter of our ongoing struggle, but rather it's how we resolve it in our life that determines victory or defeat. Four years later Paul said in Philippians, *"What you have learned and received and heard and seen in me—practice these things, and the God of peace will be with you"* (Philippians 4:9).

Before and after Paul's confessing his inner conflict, he continued to instruct others to live like he did in order to receive God's blessing in their lives. This proves that the inner "fight" between our deep feelings of inadequacy versus our willingness to remain obedient to God's will is normal. So don't live in defeat! Victory rests in believing by accepting Christ's forgiveness of all our sins, then leaving all our failures at Calvary. Because it was there all our debts were cancelled! There is no more reason left to feel down on ourselves once we realize that the blood of Jesus covers everything in our past. When we dwell on our past failures, we allow Satan to condemn us and hinder our moving forward in Christ. God never reminds us of our past because He has forgiven us of it. The Bible says He no longer remembers our sin so why would he now condemn us?

If our self-image is negative and we desire to change, begin by understanding how that poor opinion got there. Unraveling how self-image works begins with understanding how the human mind works.

While reading this chapter, remember that your mind is a part of your soul. The soul is made up of the will, the emotions, and the mind. Later we'll compare how our soul functions in relation to our self-image. The mind is a marvelous and powerful creation of God. It's like a huge memory bank that stores everything we take in through our senses. As a result of our experiences, we develop certain attitudes. In addition to forming opinions about people and events, we form opinions about ourselves based on the data entering our mental computer.

Logic tells us that if we are a good person like we're supposed to be, we can expect to be accepted and valued by others. However, when others don't embrace us as we had anticipated, we may begin to sense that maybe something is wrong with us. Consequently, the more we experience real *I know that God accepts me just as I am* rejection or even just feelings of rejection, the more likely we are to develop a low opinion of ourselves. This, in turn, fuels a self-perception of inferiority, inadequacy, or even guilt. So even if you don't believe you have a low opinion of yourself; you still may not be able to explain why at times you set minimum goals, worry about failure, and are fearful of criticism. The issue at hand is that we're oblivious to most of the "cerebral files" stored in our brains. And even though those mental records are not part of our conscious mind, subconsciously they generate unexplainable feelings and emotions.

The mind has three levels: the conscious, the preconscious, and the subconscious.

THE CONSCIOUS MIND

Picture an iceberg floating in the Arctic Ocean. Now visualize that iceberg as being your mind with the tip above the water. The part you can see above water represents your conscious mind. It includes the things we see, touch, understand, and are aware of consciously.

THE PRECONSCIOUS MIND

While you may realize there's more of the iceberg below, you can vaguely see it through the water; that part of the ice just under the waterline is like your preconscious mind. It includes responses that aren't currently conscious to you now but those you could recall with relatively little effort. For instance, if you are seated in a chair right now, you aren't consciously aware of the pressure of your body in the seat. But having just mentioned it, you can bring it into your consciousness and think about it.

Driving a car is another good example. Drivers experience all kinds of automatic motions without really thinking about them: stopping for a traffic light, signaling, and turning, etc. We do not consciously think, "Okay, I am now going to put on the brake and stop at this traffic light. I will wait here until it changes to green." It's so automatic that we do it without consciously thinking about it. Yet at any given moment, we can be consciously aware of every aspect of driving.

THE SUBCONSCIOUS MIND

Now imagine swimming under the water of this iceberg discovering the largest part far down below the surface where it is beyond our view. Although that portion is there just as surely as the rest, we're unable to see it. This massive unseen section of the iceberg represents our subconscious mind that is relatively inaccessible to us. Because we find it painful to confront the negative events in our lives and the rejection that is often associated with those experiences, we often repress them. And since we are reluctant to deal with these situations long-term basis consciously, we push them down to the levels of pre/subconsciousness. There, it's easier to get by every day not having to contend with those adversities. Without even being aware of it, often our collection of previous guilt, failure, condemnation, sin, and distress is the prime reason leading to a very poor image of ourselves. Consequently, the negative attitudes we harbor toward ourselves are expressed through our emotions rather than in our conscious mind. Therefore, these adverse feelings tend to be locked into the subconscious mind. As the Holy Spirit begins healing our negativity, we must understand and then acknowledge that it's deeply rooted there from our past. It just takes time and a great deal of patience.

I heard a story about a mother shopping at a department store with her small boy. She carefully instructed him not to open any doors, and absolutely not to talk to strangers unless she introduced them. A few minutes later distracted while shopping and lost track of her son. Suddenly, she turned around just in time as he was opening a door in the dressing area. "Stop! I told you not to open any doors!" Frightened to tears, the boy quickly stepped away from the door. *I won't ever do that again,* he thought. So his mother went back to shopping. Not too soon after that, she looked over her shoulder and saw her son was talking to a man. This time she yelled so loud that everybody in the store heard her. "I told you to never talk to strangers unless I introduce them to you!" "Yes, Mommy, the little boy sobbed, I promise that I won't ever do that again."

Unfortunately, that that little boy grew up to become a door-to-door salesman. Is it any wonder why every time he approached another house, he became so anxious that he could hardly knock on the door? He may not remember that childhood experience, but his subconscious mind will never forget it! Now it's down so deeply rooted in his subconscious, it only comes out through his feelings and emotions. Without knowing why, he feels very inadequate as a salesperson.

You may be a person who has trouble standing up in front of a roomful of people to give a talk. You find your heart pounding so strongly you can't catch your breath. You can't focus. Then your mind goes blank just as you get up to the front of the room. You feel like you're going to pass out any second! Maybe as a kid you were called on in school to give a report before a roomful of classmates. Perhaps, you stumbled along so awkwardly and were so embarrassed; you swore "never again!" Even though you don't remember many of those types of experiences, your subconscious mind does. And today, those experiences express themselves through feelings of anxiety.

My Lord Jesus Christ is the creator of everything

For the most part, what we've been discussing is how the world explains God's wonderful creation of the human mind and just how it functions. Remember though, God created our mind, but man is trying to explain it excluding Him.

Earlier we discussed the three parts to the human soul; they are the mind, the will, and the emotions. It is from within our soul that we think, feel, and act. Now let's see how these relate to what we have discussed about the mind in the previous pages.

My will, mind and emotions are under the Holy Spirit's control

As we read earlier in Romans chapter 7, Paul had an inner conflict between his new Christlike nature and his old fleshly nature. In that passage of Scripture Paul admitted he didn't understand himself. Perhaps it was because he had so many adverse encounters buried deep in his lower nature, possibly within his subconscious mind. Reflecting on Paul's recorded life, we see that he had some very troubling memories and difficult times. It's possible that his past memories haunted him. It is believed that Paul actually held the coats of the executioners as they stoned Stephen to death in Acts 7:59.

Paul was so violently opposed to the early Christian movement that he did everything he could to destroy it. *"But Saul, still breathing threats and murder against the disciples of the Lord, went to the high priest and asked him for letters to the synagogues at Damascus, so that if he found any belonging to the Way, men or women, he might bring them bound to Jerusalem"* (Acts 9:1–2).

Can you imagine how Paul, now a convert to Christ himself, must have felt when he decided to go on a new missionary journey? Emotionally he was very excited over the possibility of reaching people for Christ, making a strong decision of the will to preach the gospel at every opportunity. However, I think that there were times when his self-image suffered a great deal as he remembered all the wrong he had previously done against the cause of Christ. Paul said,

> *"For I delight in the law of God, in my inner being, but I see in my members another law waging war against the law of my mind and making me captive to the law of sin that dwells in my members"* (Romans 7:23-23).

If Paul's words were spoken using today's terminology, he might have said something like this: "I have decided to do God's will, however, there is something deep in my subconscious mind that is at war with my conscious mind. I don't understand why I can't get myself to do what I know God wants me to do. This deep anxiety makes me feel unworthy to do what God has called me to do. After all, how can I possibly overcome all the damage I've already done to the church?"

Satan will taunt us with our past sins and failures using guilt, shame, and condemnation to convince us that we are unworthy to do anything worthwhile for Christ.

JESUS HAS SET US FREE!

Paul was no different in his day than we are today! One of the most important apostles in history, struggled with the sins and failures of his past. But he knew where to turn for help. *"Who will free me from my slavery to this deadly lower nature? Thank God! It has been done by Jesus Christ our Lord. He has set me free."* Paul knew that Jesus Christ, the

Jesus has set me free from the slavery to my deadly lower nature

one who was the creator of everything, was the only one that could heal his soul. He wrote:

> *"He is the image of the invisible God, the firstborn of all creation. For by him all things were created, in heaven and on earth, visible and invisible, whether thrones or dominions or rulers or authorities—all things were created through him and for him. And he is before all things, and in him all things hold"* (Colossians 1:15-17).

Even though Paul had times when his inner thoughts and feelings were at war with his conscious decisions, he was still able to say, *"Imitate me, just as I also imitate Christ"* (I Corinthians 11:1).

Paul must have believed that God had already overcome the sins and failures of his past and that it didn't matter how he felt. He believed by faith, that Christ had paid for all his iniquities at Calvary. Paul began acknowledging what he believed to be true by faith even before he felt the difference emotionally. He didn't make his decisions based on how he felt about himself; he made his decisions based on what he knew about Christ.

Paul's self-image changed when he was able to comprehend God's unconditional love by accepting His forgiveness. Like Paul, we can do the same thing. By God's grace we can change our self-image through His Word and the power of the Holy Spirit. We must learn from God Himself who we are and what we are. Once we fully discover this, we will no longer be bound up with a low self-image.

Chapter Five

KNOW WHO YOU ARE IN CHRIST

Questions for home study and group discussion

Now that we know the truth, why do we doubt ourselves and have deep feelings of inadequacy?

How does Proverbs 23:7 answer question number one?
If we keep thinking certain _____, they will become our _____ and then our _____ and will be reflected in our _____.

What did Jesus say about believing?
Mark 9:23, Mark 11:23b, Matthew 8:13

What was Paul's answer to how he overcame the struggle he had in his lower nature?   Romans 7:15–25

Notes from My Mentor's Personal Experiences

_____
_____
_____
_____
_____
_____
_____
_____
_____
_____
_____
_____
_____
_____
_____
_____
_____
_____
_____
_____
_____
_____
_____
_____
_____

Scripture Memory **Chapter Five**

"For as a man thinks in his heart, so is he."
(Proverbs 23:7)

CHAPTER SIX

BE TRANSFORMED BY THE RENEWING OF YOUR MIND

"Do not be conformed to this world, but be transformed by the renewal of your mind, that by testing you may discern what is the will of God, what is good and acceptable and perfect." (Romans 12:2)

Through your entire life, others and especially those who influenced you in your early childhood have largely determined your self-image. Children view of themselves as a reflection of their parents' view of them. So if they told you that you were a "good child," you probably accepted their opinion. But what if they said that you were a "bad child," it's likely you believed them. Even worse, what if they told you that you never did anything right? You get my point. So much may not be true especially in light of being an impressionable child, but you likely believed it as if it had emanated from an impeccable authority.

If you are beginning to discover that you really do have a low self-image, don't condemn yourself because of it.

It's not your fault. Self-condemnation only makes the situation worse. Right now, it's important for you to accept yourself just as you are. If you are very critical of yourself, it's okay because until now you didn't know how you could be any different. And if you already have a good self-image and feel good about yourself; great! More than likely, your parents accepted, encouraged, and helped you to believe good things about yourself. That said, we could all stand to make some adjustments in our self-images.

HOW DO WE TAKE CHARGE OF THE PROGRAMMING PROCESS?

In a way, computers work like our minds. And God's Word works in conjunction with our thoughts similar to software. That software is programed to tell us who we are in Christ! So now with the help of the Holy Spirit transforming our minds by His Word, we can literally delete the "viruses" of doubt, fear, anger, hurt, resentment, lust, addictions, and condemnation. Further, we can begin reprograming what's already in process! So now let's begin to program some new thoughts into your mind. You can change.

We can develop a whole new positive attitude toward ourselves. Because we have developed adverse habit patterns in our mind due to so much negative information being fed into our mental computer. But once we decide to begin making positive acknowledgements, it's surprising when our mind continues to respond negatively. That's because we have so much undesirable data about ourselves already programmed into our mind that once a positive enters in, it's neutralized before it

I have the mind of Christ developing within me

can take effect. Here we are going to do something from now on and our mind tells us "sorry you can't do that." We feed in "Yes!" into a mind filled with "No's." Then somewhere inside the "Yes" get diluted when mixed with an overwhelming number of "No's" already there!

Have you ever made a New Year's resolution to lose weight or quit smoking? Once you're determined you are going to do it, it's as though you are standing in front of your own mental computer and programming into it: "I can do it." The computer takes your data, computes it, and gives you a read-out. But then you're amazed to read the computer's result: "You can't do it." What?! That's not what you programmed into it! How in the world did it get changed from positive to negative as it went through the computation? The change occurred because you programmed one positive thought into a mental computer crammed full of negative thoughts, values, and characteristics that have been developed over a long time. The positive thinking you generated was not accepted or recognized as a valid entry because of the negative opinion you have of yourself.

And the computer was right, or so it would seem. After trying for a few hours or maybe a few weeks to lose weight or to quit smoking, you returned to your old way of thinking. It seems so hopeless, and you eventually give up and return to your old previous behavior pattern. But to really change the entire reprogramming of your mind from negative to positive requires considerable time, practice, and perseverance. Be encouraged! You've got to keep feeding positive responses into your computer until the positive ones outweigh the negative ones. Eventually the time and effort will pay off.

One day you will notice the computer's readout and it will say, "Well, maybe you can do it." Now you are almost there! Keep pouring in the positives and your persistence will be rewarded when your mental computer reads, "Yes, you're right, you can do it." Congratulations! You've begin to discover that you really can do it! Your new positive attitude will begin producing positive results that change your life. First, you'll begin to believe that you really can be successful at what you want to do. Next, you'll start accepting that you're truly capable of doing anything God wants you to do. Finally, you'll be putting your faith into action and getting it accomplished.

ACT THE WAY CHRIST WOULD ACT IN EVERY SITUATION

In the introduction of "Spiritual Characteristics of a Godly Life," I explained that our purpose in life should be to "conform to the image of Christ." That means that our goal is to eventually act the way Christ would behave in every situation we encounter in our daily lives. In order to accomplish this, we must first ensure that our principles are in line with Christ. Remember that our values become our character and our character is reflected in our behavior. If our desire is to act the way Christ would act, we must first think the way Christ thinks.

In Philippians it says, *"Have this mind among yourselves, which is yours in Christ Jesus"* (Phil. 2:5) The only way to have the mind of Christ is to make His Word so much a part of our thinking that we automatically respond to His principles and adopt His values as our own. As we acknowledge His Word as truth in all we do, we'll begin to walk in the fullness of the authority He has given us in His name.

CONFESSION IS GOOD FOR THE SOUL

It's said, "Confession is good for the soul." This is very true. The word "confession" means to acknowledge or to agree with. Therefore, I would like to make a slight modification to this statement, "Positive acknowledgement is good for the soul."

A positive acknowledgement is a verbal statement affirming what God is working in our lives. Because we're in verbal agreement with God, that declaration fortifies our beliefs and trust that God will do exactly what He says that He will do. In stark contrast, when we surrender to doubt and fear with a negative acknowledgement, we're actually denying what God has promised He is doing in our lives. And remember that in order to confirm our salvation, the Bible states that we must profess with our mouths that Christ died for our sins and that God raised Him from the grave. Therefore, what we believe in our heart has to be expressed with our mouth.

> *"But what does it say? "The word is near you, in your mouth and in your heart" (that is, the word of faith that we proclaim); because, if you confess with your mouth that Jesus is Lord and believe in your heart that God raised him from the dead, you will be saved. For with the heart one believes and is justified, and with the mouth one confesses and is saved"* (Romans 10:8–10).

WE WILL BE JUDGED BY OUR WORDS

Jesus said that we will be judged by our words, either unto justification or condemnation.

"The good person out of his good treasure brings forth good, and the evil person out of his evil treasure brings forth evil. I tell you, on the day of judgment people will give account for every careless word they speak, for by your words you will be justified, and by your words you will be condemned" (Matthew 12:35–37).

I fix my thoughts on what is good and right

Jesus also said:

"So everyone who acknowledges me before men, I also will acknowledge before my Father who is in heaven, but whoever denies me before men, I also will deny before my Father who is in heaven" (Matthew 10: 32–33).

Our spoken words are very important to God. Because He's creator, He knows that the words from our mouths are a direct reflection of the intents and thoughts of our heart. If we desire God's blessing, our words must be consistent with His Word and His promises. God's Word is positive, creative, healing, life-giving, kind, unselfish, and true. But the Kingdom of this world is destructive, wounding, life-taking, cruel, narcissistic, and deceitful. Therefore, don't be conformed to this world by its negativity, but "be transformed by the renewing of your mind" in God's Word.

Jesus said that we will have what we say

"And Jesus answered them, "Have faith in God. Truly, I say to you, whoever says to this mountain, 'Be taken up and thrown into the sea,' and does not doubt in his heart, but

*believes that what he says will come to pass, it
will be done for him. Therefore, I tell you,
whatever you ask in prayer, believe that you
have received it, and it will be yours"*
(Mark 11:22–24).

Jesus places a vital emphasis on we say, *"whatever you
ask in prayer, believe that you have received it, and it will be yours."* At
creation, God simply spoke and the world was put in place.
Because we are made in the image of God our words can also
be creative and life-giving. Above, Mark 11:23 said that we
would have whatever we speak providing we don't doubt.
Acknowledgement is speaking out loud the things we believe
will happen. Conversely, even now our negative words and
emotions greatly dampen the flame of our life's purpose in
Christ. In Matthew 12:36, we read that you must give account
on the day of judgment for every idle word spoken. Those
words can be negative words of unbelief, and doubt is not
from God.

WE MUST AGREE TOGETHER

The most powerful form of acknowledgement
happens when two or more people truly agree together on
something. *"Again, I say to you, if two of you agree on earth about
anything they ask, it will be done for them by my Father in heaven. For
where two or three are gathered in my name, there am I among them"*
(Matthew 18:19–20). God always tells the truth! He said that
if we say anything and believe it in our heart without doubt,
we have it. He goes on to say that if two of us will agree upon

anything, we will have that also. This is especially exciting for husbands and wives who are willing to agree together in prayer for the things they believe.

God has promised that He will supply all our needs according to His riches in glory by Christ Jesus. So how can we live in this authority if we refuse to acknowledge that we believe God's Word? We need to start confessing that our needs are met before we can see the results. By doing this, we are walking by faith, not by sight. Even though the world worries about the future, we can trust God to take care our tomorrows. We know that when we're in agreement with God's Word, it is as good as done. Therefore, it's our part to believe God by acting in faith for what we ask. It's God's job to bring about the results according to His plans, not ours. Knowing His Word and then trusting Him to do accordingly to His will.

Finally, let me leave a word of inspiration for all you "doubting Thomas's." In John 20:24–29 Jesus already knew Thomas was filled with disbelief after his death but made a special visit to dispel that doubt and comfort in his heart. Remember also, that before Christ ascended to Heaven, He promised us the "comforter" which is written specifically about in the chapter 19 of John.

> *Having Christ in my heart is my only hope of glory*

HOW DOES ACKNOWLEDGMENT DIFFER FROM AUTO-SUGGESTION?

Isn't acknowledgment just another way of saying "auto-suggestion?" Although there are some similarities; the differences are important. "Auto-suggestion" primarily uses our own voice to program positive affirmations into our mind. Taught by some behavioral scientists: that as you repeat instructions to yourself; your mind more quickly responds. They encourage patients to read positive assertions out loud several times daily. However, acknowledgment I'm discussing here is positive affirmation based on faith in God's Word. Our belief is that what God says in His Word is true even though I can't see the results at this time. Our foundation of authority is that God does not lie and what He says must come to pass. The power in this vocal acknowledgement is that what I believe God says about me is true. And though I may not feel worthy of it, I recognize something will happen regardless if there's no material evidence... until it happens.

So if we go back to the concept of our mind being like a mental computer, how does this all relate? Simple! If we repeat the Word of God over and over acknowledging that it is true, we are hiding it in our own heart. The psalmist said:

I am delighted in God's Word. I will remember it forever.

"How can a young man keep his way pure? By guarding it according to your word. With my whole heart, I seek you; let me not wander from your commandments! I have stored up your word in my heart, that I might not sin against you. Blessed are you, O LORD; teach me your statutes! With my lips I declare all the rules of your mouth. In the way of your testimonies I delight as much as in all riches. I will meditate on your precepts and fix my eyes on your ways. I will delight in your statutes; I will not forget your word" (Psalm 119:9–16).

By acknowledging God's Word aloud, we are feeding His thoughts into our mind. Eventually, God's thoughts will become our thoughts, and then His values will become our values. Then once we completely accept God's values about us, we will fully realize that we are people of extreme value. Recognizing His very special plan for us fuels our passion for living for Him! Knowing God personally and holding what He says about us close to our hearts; we will realize that all the negatives once believed about ourselves no longer have a bearing on in our future.

GOD'S THOUGHTS BECOME OUR THOUGHTS

By transforming our mind and our thoughts through positive acknowledgment by the declaration with our lips, we're hiding God's Word in our heart in faith. So if you haven't sincerely begun hiding God's Word by instilling it in your thoughts, may I encourage you to do so! As God told Joshua to meditate on the Word daily, Paul tells us to: *"Finally, brothers, whatever is true, whatever is honorable, whatever is just, whatever is pure, whatever is lovely, whatever is commendable, if there is any excellence, if there is anything worthy of praise, think about these things"* (Philippians 4:8) In the Living Bible it says, *"Fix your thoughts on what is true and good and right. Think about things that are pure and lovely, and dwell on the fine, good things in others. Think about all you can praise God for and be glad about."*

The beginning of transformation is changing your thought life. The things we think about over and over will become our values. Guard your heart. Be diligent about what you're watching or what entertainment you're participating in. Be careful what you read and the materials you're focusing your time on. You've heard the old saying, "Garbage in, garbage out." If we are to think as Christ thinks we need to put His thoughts into our mind over and over. They become our thoughts, our values, our character, and then our behavior. Keep your mental computer filled with positive!

HOW DOES A CHRISTIAN OBTAIN A GOOD SELF IMAGE?

1. Knowing God's love
    God showed how much He loved us by sending His only Son into this fallen world to bring to us eternal life through Jesus. In His death, we see what real love is. It's not our love for God, but His love for us when He sent His Son to pay our ransom and satisfy God's anger against our sins.

    God's mighty power is at work within me doing more than I could ever ask or dream.

    "So we have come to know and to believe the love that God has for us. God is love, and whoever abides in love abides in God, and God abides in him. By this is love perfected with us, so that we may have confidence for the day of judgment, because as he is so also are we in this world. There is no fear in love, but perfect love casts out fear. For fear has to do with punishment, and whoever fears has not been perfected in love. We love because he first loved us" (I John 4:16–19).

2. Knowing our position

    "For you did not receive the spirit of slavery to fall back into fear, but you have received the Spirit of adoption as sons, by whom we cry, "Abba! Father!" The Spirit himself bears witness with our spirit that we are children of God, and if children, then heirs—heirs of God and fellow heirs with Christ, provided we suffer with him in order that we may also be glorified with him" (Romans 8:15–17).

3. Knowing who Christ is

    "Therefore, God has highly exalted him and bestowed on him the name that is above every name, so that at the name of Jesus every knee should bow, in heaven and on earth and under the earth, and every tongue confess that Jesus Christ is Lord, to the glory of God the Father" (Philippians 2:9-11).

4. Knowing we have eternal life

    "Whoever believes in the Son of God has the testimony in himself. Whoever does not believe God has made him a liar, because he has not believed in the testimony that God has borne concerning his Son. And this is the testimony, that God gave us eternal life, and this life is in his Son. Whoever has the Son has life; whoever does not have the Son of God does not have life. I write these things to you who believe in the name of the Son of God that you may know that you have eternal life" (I John 5:10–13).

5. Knowing who lives in us

   "And this is the secret: 'To them God chose to make known how great among the Gentiles are the riches of the glory of this mystery, which is Christ in you, the hope of glory'" (Colossians 1:27). *"In that day you will know that I am in my Father, and you in me, and I in you" (John 14:20). "Little children, you are from God and have overcome them, for he who is in you is greater than he who is in the world"* (I John 4:4).

WHAT CAN WE EXPECT AS A RESULT OF CHRIST'S LIFE IN US?

1. Redemption and forgiveness

   "In him we have redemption through his blood, the forgiveness of our trespasses, according to the riches of his grace" (Ephesians 1:7).

2. Strength and love

   "That according to the riches of his glory he may grant you to be strengthened with power through his Spirit in your inner being, so that Christ may dwell in your hearts through faith—that you, being rooted and grounded in love, may have strength to

   My only power and success comes from God.

comprehend with all the saints what is the breadth and length and height and depth, and to know the love of Christ that surpasses knowledge, that you may be filled with all the fullness of God. Now to him who is able to do far more abundantly than all that we ask or think, according to the power at work within us" (Ephesians 3:16–20).

3. Confidence and sufficiency
   "Such is the confidence that we have through Christ toward God. Not that we are sufficient in ourselves to claim anything as coming from us, but our sufficiency is from God" (II Corinthians 3:4–5).

4. Joy and peace
   "Rejoice in the Lord always; again, I will say, rejoice. Do not be anxious about anything, but in everything by prayer and supplication with thanksgiving let your requests be made known to God. And the peace of God, which surpasses all understanding, will guard your hearts and your minds in Christ Jesus" (Philippians 4:4, 6–7).

> *I don't worry about anything, instead, I pray about everything*

5. Power, love, and a sound mind
   "God gave us a spirit not of fear but of power and love and self-control" (II Timothy 1:7).

Chapter Six

BE TRANSFORMED BY THE RENEWING OF YOUR MIND

Questions for home study and group discussion

Why should we be transformed by the renewing of our minds?   Romans 12:2

What must we do first in order to act the way Christ would act in any given situation?   Philippians 2:5

What is positive acknowledgement? (Answer to this question is in the text.)

What is negative acknowledgement? (Answer to this question is in the text.)

Why are the words we speak so important?
Matthew 12:35-37, Mark 11:22–24

Notes from My Mentor's Personal Experiences

_____
_____
_____
_____
_____
_____
_____
_____
_____
_____
_____
_____
_____
_____
_____
_____
_____
_____
_____
_____
_____
_____
_____
_____

Scripture Memory Chapter Six

"Do not be conformed to this world, but be transformed by the renewal of your mind, that by testing you may discern what is the will of God, what is good and acceptable and perfect."
(Romans 12:2)

CHAPTER SEVEN

YOU ARE OF EXTREME VALUE IN CHRIST

"Have this mind among yourselves, which is yours in Christ Jesus." (Philippians 2:5)

Jesus said that we are to love our neighbor, as we love ourselves. So if we don't love ourselves we're going to have a difficult experience loving others. But the important thing to remember is that no matter whom you are or what you have done, God loves you. And nothing can separate you from His love.

> *"For I am sure that neither death nor life, nor angels nor rulers, nor things present nor things to come, nor powers, nor height nor depth, nor anything else in all creation, will be able to separate us from the love of God in Christ Jesus our Lord"* (Romans 8:38–39).

GOD USES PEOPLE TO HELP US LEARN TO ACCEPT OURSELVES

The year before I entered high school, my parents decided to remarry and bring all of us younger children back to live with them again in Artesia, California. I found myself living in a house with a mother I hated and a father who was a stranger to me. I didn't feel loved by either of them. Everything about my home life left me feeling I was not worthwhile to them.

As I faced Artesia High School with fear and uncertainty, suddenly there came a new influence into my life. My high school principal Bill Atkins took an active interest in me. Every time he saw me, which was quite often, he would say, "Roy, you can be anything you want to be! You're intelligent, capable, and can have anything in this world you want." But I really thought he was crazy because I was sure he said those things because he didn't really know what I was really like. And besides, he didn't know what my home was like. Regardless of those things he kept saying, "Roy, you can be anything you want to be." Later I found out that he knew all about me and still believed I could be anything I wanted to be.

As high school went on, I came to the conclusion: "He's really a smart man. If he says I can be anything I want to be, maybe he's right." Mr. Atkins encouraged me in everything I did getting me involved in many student activities. Before I knew it, I was active in campus politics and elected to our community youth coordinating council. Afterward I was selected for the county of Los Angeles Youth Coordinating Council. I later became a member of the youth coordinating council for the state of California and served on the governor's youth advisory committee.

I was able to accomplish all this because one man took an interest in me. All through high school Principal Bill Atkins encouraged me, "Roy, you can be anything you want to be."

Although flourishing during the day in high school, returning home at night I still faced the same old fears and loneliness. Consequently, I began running the streets with a gang called "The Sinners" and soon thereafter, distinguished myself enough to become their president. There I was president of the youth coordinating council during the day and a hoodlum by night! I was leading two completely opposite lives and it was tearing me apart on the inside. During the summer before my senior year, I got into trouble with the police. So entering my last year in high school, I did some soul searching.

In spite my legal trouble, Mr. Atkins never lost faith in me when I was down. That meant everything to me! Instead, he continued to inspire me and helped me accept myself. He went on to say anyone could get into trouble and told me he knew I would not have behaved that way under normal circumstances. Mr. Atkins assured me that he was confident I would never do it again. And just like before, he went right on telling me I could be anything I wanted to be. More than ever, I began to accept myself as a person of value. What a change that brought in my self-image and my life! Because of that I could accept myself and was able to offer that same acceptance to others. Mr. Atkins had reprogrammed positive thoughts about who I was into my mental computer previously crammed full of negativity my entire life. Oh, it took time, but my attitude about myself began to change. Then as my attitude changed, my actions and my life changed.

Although you may not have a Mr. Atkins in your life feeding positive perspective into your mind about yourself; you do have God's Word. Even if there is nothing else, God's

Word is all the reinforcement your heart and mind require to help you see yourself as God sees you. You are a child of the King, a joint heir with Christ because you know Him as your personal Savior. But remember there's even more! Jesus promised us the Holy Spirit "comforter" to guide and direct us

I trust and obey God in everything.

REPLACE NEGATIVE ACKNOWLEDGMENTS WITH POSITIVE ONES

Negative Acknowledgments: "How things can't be done, because of fear, doubt, and worry."

Positive Acknowledgment: "How things are already done according to God's Word." The Word of God is our most powerful instrument for changing how we feel about ourselves.

Our purpose in life is to "conform to the image of Christ" (Romans 8:29). That means that our goal is to eventually act the way Christ would act in every situation we encounter in our daily lives. To realize this, we must first ensure that our values are lined up with Christ's. If we are to act the way Christ would act, we need to think the way Christ thinks. *"Have this mind among yourselves, which is yours in Christ Jesus"* (Philippians 2:5).

Therefore, the only way to have the mind of Christ is to ingrain His Word so much into our thinking that we automatically respond to His values and adopt them as our own. As we acknowledge His Word as truth, our minds are rejuvenated, and our lives are transformed.

"How can a young man keep his way pure? By guarding it according to your word. I have stored up your word in my heart, that I might not sin against you." (Psalms 119:9, 11).

> *"Do not be conformed to this world, but be transformed by the renewal of your mind, that by testing you may discern what is the will of God, what is good and acceptable and perfect"* (Romans 12:2).

As I've emphasized many times, values begin with thoughts. Repeating thoughts over and over, gradually we begin to believe them. Once we accept them, they become our values. Our values then form our character. Eventually we act out these characteristics through our behavior. Consequently, our actions directly reflect what we permit ourselves to think about over and over.

The writer of Proverbs says, *"For as he thinks in his heart, so is he"* (Proverbs 23:7, KJV) He is telling us that what we think about deep within our heart is what we become.

The Process of Transformation

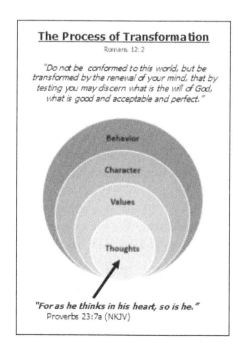

The Apostle Paul said, *"Set your mind on things above"* (Colossians 3:2).

He also said, *"Fix your thoughts on what is true and good and right. Think about things that are pure and lovely and dwell on the fine, good things in others. Think about all you can praise God for and be glad about"* (Philippians 4:8, TLB) and *"Be renewed in the spirit of your mind"* (Ephesians 4:20–24).

> *"For though we walk in the flesh, we are not waging war according to the flesh. For the weapons of our warfare are not of the flesh but have divine power to destroy strongholds. We destroy arguments and every lofty opinion raised against the knowledge of God and take every thought captive to obey Christ"* (II Corinthians 10:3–5).

This Scripture tells us how to have victory in our thoughts. Our tool is so powerful that it brings down strongholds, *arguments*, and every high thing that exalts itself against the knowledge of God.

I have set my mind on things above.

"Strongholds" are those things in our lives that have a hold on us. Things like fear, lust, and past failures that continually haunt us. Other crippling strongholds such as doubt, bitterness, hatred, and negativity keep us from expressing our love for God or others.

What do most of us do when we are in those moments of doubt and fear? We imagine everything that can go wrong. II Corinthians 10:5 KJV speaks of *"casting down imaginations and every lofty opinion raised against the knowledge of God and take every thought captive to obey Christ."*

That same verse in the English Standard Version refers to "casting down arguments." So when we are facing doubt we seldom think about how things can go right. Its then, we must be able to cast down those arguments and imaginations before they defeat us or possibly destroy us. And, we have the means available to us of doing just that.

Every high thing that exalts itself against the knowledge of God; the things of the world are against the knowledge of God. Some of the thoughts we continuously turn over in our minds are against the knowledge of God. Therefore, we need to stop engaging in the world's thinking and replace it with God's thinking.

The way to have victory is to bring every thought into captivity to the obedience of Christ. We have the choice as to whether or not we're going to surrender our thoughts to the obedience of Christ. It is our responsibility to obey God's Word.

I do not allow my thoughts to exalt themselves against the knowledge of God.

How do we get rid of our old thinking and replace it with new thinking? We accomplish that through the Principle of Displacement.

The Principle of Displacement

One way of illustrating this displacement process is using a big bucket of hot, black coffee. Suppose someone tells you to change the hot black coffee into cold clear water without pouring it out. Now picture an unlimited supply of ice cubes but you can only put a single ice cube in that bucket of hot coffee at a time. In this demonstration, the bucket of black coffee represents the negative habit patterns already programmed into your mind. In contrast, the ice cubes are the positive acknowledgements you are now programing into your mental computer. Before getting started, however, make sure to take the container of hot coffee off the heat or the water will never get cold! So now what happens to the black coffee when you put just one ice cube into it? Nothing! What happens if you put a second? Now put in a 3rd? Probably nothing!

But if you stand there long enough putting in ice cubes, one at a time, into that bucket of hot black coffee;

eventually it will spill over. Soon thereafter it will begin to cool down and get lighter in color. After a very long while, patiently adding ice cubes to the bucket, the black coffee will be completely displaced with cold, clear water. The same principle is true with our minds. Because we have built up negative mental habit patterns making it very difficult for us to accept positive acknowledgements about ourselves; it's tough for us to believe we can be as successful as we want to be. But every time you tell yourself "I can" instead of "I can't," you're placing another ice cube in that bucket of black coffee.

"This Book of the Law shall not depart out of your mouth, but you shall meditate on it day and night, that you may observe and do according to all that is written in it. For then you shall make your way prosperous, and then you shall deal wisely and have good success" (Joshua 1:8) When we obey the Word of God it brings prosperity, wisdom, and good success. Before Joshua took over the leadership of the Children of Israel, he was instructed how to be successful in the task ahead. That's why once we comprehend the power of God's Word, we'll begin to see why God teaches us to meditate on it and then obey that which it instructs us.

The only way I know to change an individual's behavior is by changing their values. As godly people our purpose is to conform to the image of Christ. Therefore, the only way to conform to His image is to make His values our own by hiding His Word in our hearts! If we spend the majority of our life dwelling on worldly thinking, we'll end up thinking just like the world. But if we invest our time studying God's Word, we are transformed by the Word. It all starts with what we think about and hide deep in our hearts.

Once we have hidden God's Word in our hearts, we will begin to think God's thoughts.

> *"For the Word of God speaks and is alive and full of power [making it active, operative, energizing, and effective]; it is sharper than any two-edged sword, penetrating to the dividing line of the breath of life (soul) and [the immortal] spirit, and of joints and marrow [of the deepest parts of our nature], exposing and sifting and analyzing and judging the very thoughts and purposes of the heart."* (Hebrews 4:12, AMP).

In Mentoring His Way Volume 1, in the chapter on "A Life of His Word," I talked about God's Word is to be worn like a piece of armor to defeat Satan. I want to revisit that subject here. "The Word of God," what a powerful statement that is! These are the Words of God the Father, God the Son, and God the Holy Spirit. The Triune God speaks to you and me through His Word. This is not a book like any other book that just gives instructions or information. It is the living voice of God almighty speaking to us through the Bible.

There are fourteen descriptive words in this verse that begin to explain the Word of God. For the Word of God:

1. Speaks   and is
2. Alive   making it
3. Powerful
4. Active
5. Operative
6. Energizing

7. Effective   it is
8. Sharper   than any two-edged sword
9. Penetrating   to the
10. Dividing   line of the breath of life (soul) and
                         (the immortal) spirit, and the joints
                         and marrow (of the deepest parts of
                         our nature)
11. Exposing
12. Sifting
13. Analyzing
14. Judging   (discerning) the very thoughts and
                         purposes (intents) of the heart

Many theologians believe that "purposes or intents of our heart" is not talking about the heart in our chest, but it is talking about what holds the soul and the spirit together in one unit. "Jesus came into your heart" means that He came into your mind, will, emotions, and spirit. The Sword of the Spirit can cut through the deepest parts of our nature. What does the Word do when it gets down there?

God's Word "speaks and is alive." God is alive in us so that when we read the Word it becomes alive in us also. Then it goes on to say that "it is powerful." I've read a lot of things that certainly didn't seem very powerful to me. But this particular Scripture promises us that the God who created everything is speaking to us through His Word because "it is alive and powerful." These are not just normal words, but these are dynamic words that have been written to do something powerful in our lives.

I will meditate on and obey God's Word.

It is "active," it's "proactive," it goes after the things in our lives that need to be rearranged or displaced. It also says that it is "operative." This makes me think of a person in surgery. During the operation, something is being removed or repaired. The surgeon is searching for the cause of disease making the patient sick. Once found, it's eliminated. And it is "energizing!" The Word of God energizes us because it speaks and is alive, powerful, active, and operative. It is also "effective," which means that it does what it is supposed to do.

It is "sharper" than any two-edged sword. During New Testament times, a sword was the sharpest weapon available. Armed with a two-edged sword a soldier then could cut both ways and nothing could escape its sharp blade. Remember Ephesians 6 describes one of the pieces of armor as the "Sword of the Spirit, which is the Word of God." The Word of God is a sword in the hands of the Holy Spirit. So if we are filled with the Holy Spirit allowing Him to empower us, then take God's Word and put it into His hands as a sword! He is able to go in and cut out the strongholds that are constantly defeating us. In Romans 8:26, it says that when we don't know how to pray, the Holy Spirit intercedes for us according to the will of God the Father. He uses the Word of God to go in and cut out those things we can't deal with on our own, like past memories causing us to be afraid. The Word begins removing all that causes us to doubt ourselves. It is "penetrating." That means that the Holy Spirit's sword is so sharp it's able to cut out previous negative thoughts and replace them with His thoughts. It is "dividing," penetrating to the dividing line of the breath of life (soul), and (the immortal) spirit. It "exposes" what should not be there, lets us know what it is, and brings it up and lets us be aware of it so that it can be cut out.

The Word "sifts" our thoughts. Have you ever panned for gold? Typically, by dipping a pan into a sandy stream one begins sifting the contents of the pan gently back and forth to separate and eliminate the rocks and sand from the gold pieces. Somewhat like sifting wheat or other grains from the kernel using a screen. Likewise, the Scriptures above tell us that the Word sifts out the bad stuff and keeping the good. Next, it "analyzes." After a gold miner finds gold he takes it in to be analyzed to determine its quality.

Finally, it "judges." It judges the thoughts and intents of our heart in order to determine their value. Therefore, judging determines the value placed on something. In a contest, a judge determines the significance of something before awarding a prize. He gives a first prize, second prize, etc. So my desire is that when the Word of God judges my thoughts, those thoughts will have created values that are developing the character of Christ in me.

WORDPOWER – A POWERFUL METHOD OF DISPLACEMENT

Sometimes there's too much of the Word to take one in in one setting. What's worked for my wife Sarah and I is to take little pieces of Scripture and repeat them over and over. In other words, meditate on them day and night. In the next chapter, we'll hear from Sarah as she tells her story.

Instead of ice cubes in our previous example, I am using a principle that I call WordPower—using God's Word through the power of the Holy Spirit. We need to understand that the Holy Spirit is using His Sword to cut through the deepest parts of our nature displacing our deep-rooted bad habit patterns. I've taken portions of Scripture

The Word of God cuts deep into my lower nature and eliminates the things that cause me to doubt God.

and paraphrased them in the first-person present tense addressing each area of my life where I sense a need to overcome some past or present temptation, failure, or weakness. I made a list here of some of the WordPower statements that I use below.

I praise God for everything.

Christ's stripes heal me.

I trust and obey God in everything.

God provides for all my needs.

God so loved me that He gave.

Eternal life is a free gift.

I honor Christ with every part of my body.

I am a joint heir with Christ.

I bring every thought captive to the obedience of Christ.

I fix my thoughts on what is good.

I have Christ's authority over all the enemy's power.

I am transformed into Christlikeness.

I have set my mind on things above.

I serve Christ in the workplace.

I only think about the good things in others.

I wear the full armor of God.

I am Christ-actualized not self-actualized.

I can do all things through Christ.

I serve others; I do not expect them to serve me.

In Christ, I am of extreme value.

I have put to death the desires of the flesh.

Jesus loves me.

God is love.

I am controlled and empowered by the Holy Spirit.

I know Jesus as my Lord and Savior.

I love my family more than I love myself.

I hide God's Word in my heart.

I live Christ's life on purpose, not by accident.

DEVELOPING YOUR OWN WORDPOWER

Here is an example of how to develop your own WordPower statements. The Bible tells us that Jesus gave us a new commandment, *"A new commandment I give to you, that you love one another: just as I have loved you, you also are to love one another"* (John 13:34). First John chapter four is a good place to start learning how to love others. The Scriptures that are underlined and not italicized are the ones that I used to make my WordPower statements.

> *"Beloved,* let us love one another, *for* love is from God, *and* whoever loves has been born of God *and knows God. Anyone who does not love does not know God, because* God is love. *In this the love of God was made manifest among us, that God sent his only Son into the world, so that we might live through him.* In this is love, not that we have loved God but that he loved us *and sent his Son to be the propitiation for our sins. Beloved,* if God so loved us, we also ought to love one another. *No one has ever seen God; if we love one another,* God abides in us and his love is perfected in us.*"* (I John 4:7–12).

- I practice loving others.
- Love comes from God.
- Because I am loving and kind it shows that I am born of God.
- God is love.

- I love God because He loved me first.
- Since God loves me so much it causes me to love others.
- God's love within me is growing stronger.

> "*So* we have come to know and to believe the love that God has for us. *God is love, and whoever abides in love abides in God, and God abides in him.* By this is love perfected with us, *so that we may have confidence for the day of judgment, because as he is so also are we in this world. There is no fear in love, but* perfect love casts out fear. *For fear has to do with punishment, and whoever fears has not been perfected in love.* We love because he first loved us" (I John 4:16–19).

In Christ, I am a person of extreme value.

- I have come to know how much God loves.
- I am living in love therefore I am living in God.
- The God of love is living in me.
- As I live with Christ, my love grows more perfect and complete.
- I can face God with confidence.
- He loves me and I love Him too.
- His perfect love for me eliminates all dread of what He might do to me.
- My love for Him comes from Him loving me first.

161

PUT A LID ON IT!

We have a great responsibility to others to keep negative thoughts about them out of our minds. That's because we are to encourage others, not discourage them! Satan is the one who disheartens, not Jesus. What would happen if every time you put a WordPower statement of positive acknowledgment into your bucket of black coffee, someone else dumped another cup of black coffee into your bucket? How would you ever change the coffee to cold clear water? Therefore, we must learn to control what goes into our mind.

There are two parts to this equation: First, we need to turn off the fire from underneath the bucket by changing our environment. We have to stop frequenting the same places and hanging around with people of poor character who influence us toward the wrong thinking. We need to eliminate media or entertainment that poorly affects our values to prevent Satan from polluting our minds with negative acknowledgements. Second, we need to put a lid on our bucket! That lid represents the decision to refuse undesirable thoughts to enter into our mind or negative acknowledgments to come out of our mouths. Thus, we bring every thought captive to the obedience of Christ.

Remember! What we allow to enter our mind will eventually become a part of us; because we become what we think about. Once negative thinking becomes a part of us, we begin to express it with our words. And, those words become our negative acknowledgments.

If someone came into your home with a huge container of rotten smelly garbage, then dumped it on your beautiful new carpet... What would you do? Would you passively stand by? I don't think so. You wouldn't allow anyone to do that to your home! So why would you allow anyone to dump garbage in your head?

Use your Shield of Faith to block Satan's attempt at giving you his stinking thinking!

PARENTS: HELP YOUR CHILDREN TO LOVE THEMSELVES

Teach your children they are worthwhile and they're the children of God. Demonstrate how much they are loved by Him, and that they are loved very much by you. Children will generally accept your opinion of them as the truth, so make sure you tell them about themselves according to what God says about them. Children are most likely to develop their self-image according what their parents program into them by words and actions. So I'm urging you to help them accept themselves as extremely valuable individuals through your unconditional loving affirmation *"But Jesus said, "Let the little children come to me and do not hinder them, for to such belongs the kingdom of heaven"* (Matthew 19:14).

> *"And calling to him a child, he put him in the midst of them and said, "Truly, I say to you, unless you turn and become like children, you will never enter the kingdom of heaven. Whoever humbles himself like this child is the greatest in the kingdom of heaven. Whoever receives one such child in my name receives me, but whoever causes one of these little ones who believe in me to sin, it would be better for him to have a great millstone fastened around his neck and to be drowned in the depth of the sea"* (Matthew 18:2–6).

As parents, we have a great responsibility to our children to make sure that we are giving them the best possible opportunity to grow up into mature self-respecting adults. The best possible way is to teach them how very much God loves them. And because God loves them so much, they have every right as a child of God, to love themselves. Never withhold love from your children as punishment. Teach them that love is unconditional. They are loved because of their position in your family, not because they are good or bad. Show them how to create WordPower statements for themselves.

BE A WORDPOWER DEPOSITOR

Make a habit of placing WordPower in other people's buckets. In Philippians 4:8, it says that we are to think of the good things in others. So look for the things that are good in others and praise them. Please don't waste your valuable time thinking or talking about the bad in others. Most people already know what's wrong within them. But most of us need to be reminded of our good qualities. I used to work for a man who told me to look for the good in everybody. He said, "After you find something good, even if it's only that he tied his shoes properly, praise that until you find something else that is worth praising." He said that eventually I would be surprised at how much good I could find in the least possible candidate. After only practicing this awhile I found out how true it was. All I have to do is remember how Mr. Atkins treated me throughout my high school years.

By depositing WordPower acknowledgments into others, we can help them until they're able to accept themselves enough to take over the programming on their own. Look for good and praise it!

But when there's bad—forgive it! Then forget about it! Like Jesus taught us: to treat others the way we would want to be treated. Using this example: speak only good things about others because that's exactly how you'd want them to talk about you!

Chapter Seven

YOU ARE OF EXTREME VALUE IN CHRIST

Questions for home study and group discussion

If God thinks so much of us, how can we continue to think so little of ourselves?   Romans 8:38–39

How can we learn to think more like Christ?
Romans 12:2, Philippians 2:5, 4:8

How can we replace negative acknowledgements with positive acknowledgements? (Answer to this question is in the text.)

How do we put a lid on our bucket?
II Corinthians 10:3–5

How can you help your children learn to love themselves in Christ?   Matthew 19:14, 18:2–6

Notes from My Mentor's Personal Experiences

_____

_____

_____

_____

_____

_____

_____

_____

_____

_____

_____

_____

_____

_____

_____

_____

_____

_____

_____

_____

_____

_____

_____

_____

Scripture Memory Chapter Seven

_"Have this mind among yourselves, which is
yours in Christ Jesus."_ (Philippians 2:5)

CHAPTER EIGHT

WORDPOWER IN ACTION

"Brothers, I do not consider that I have made it my own. But one thing I do: forgetting what lies behind and straining forward to what lies ahead." (Philippians 3:13-14)

I have spoken many times about what happened to me when I was sent to prison. But too often, my wife Sarah's story gets left out of the conversation even though she had a more difficult time than I did. In fact, it was Sarah who first discovered WordPower. The following is Sarah telling her story to the women's fellowship at our church. Let's listen in and hear Sarah's perspective.

THE SARAH COMSTOCK STORY

I have a twofold reason for being here to share with you today:

First, I have a message I want to bring to you. But that message will come after I tell you a story today of how Satan attacked my husband and I and how God loved us through it all.

The second reason is more personal because the very act of sharing these events brings light and understanding to the whole thing. And when we bring a situation out in the open and into the light of God's grace, then God can take what was meant for harm and turn it into blessing. So if someone here today is encouraged by something I say, then it serves to eliminate the sting of what the enemy intended me to feel when I remember our story.

Although this story is not the message, I must tell you what happened to Roy and I before I can actually share how it affected me as a woman. There are a multitude of side stories stemming from our experience; and so many of them are intense, suspenseful, and inspirational, with a whole lot of other adjectives. But I don't want to get sidetracked from the real message.

This one thing I do; Forgetting those things which are behind.

The lifestyle I married into was very different from what I had ever experienced before. Roy was in the process of purchasing a large, three-story house that he had been leasing. The entire top floor was the master's bedroom built over an indoor racquetball court. Additionally, we had two housekeepers coming each week to take care of it all. For his business use, Roy had two limousines at his disposal at any time. They're really quite handy when grocery shopping, especially with a driver to carry the bags! Roy took me to all the best restaurants in Los Angeles, including Beverly Hills. He treated me like a princess on a pedestal—like a fairy tale come true!

When Roy and I married on April 12, 1985, he was the CEO of his own multimillion-dollar financial services corporation. Starting the company from his kitchen table, within three years it became very prosperous employing over two hundred people. Roy had vice presidents running four divisions: insurance, real estate services, tax and accounting, and investments. His own background and expertise was in the insurance area, so he hired key executives for each division and trusted them to be experts in their fields.

When we returned from our beautiful month-long honeymoon in Hawaii, Japan, and Hong Kong in May 1985, the Securities & Exchange Commission (SEC) came to Roy's office to investigate a very rapidly growing investment program that was being sold through the company. Their initial findings stated that the plan should have been registered and licensed with the SEC, but it had not been registered at the advice of the vice president of the investment division and his legal counsel. As the SEC investigated the program further, much bigger problems than the registration issue came to light. Investment funds had been covertly moved into a company owned by that vice president and then subsequently transferred out of the country. Ultimately, Roy was hit with the information that millions of dollars had been "miss-directed" as the summer of 1985 was consumed with endless meetings with the SEC, lawyers, that vice president, and more lawyers! Even though that vice president was able to return a portion of the money, the rest had already been turned over to, I'll call him the *"Deceiver,"* who initially brought this "too good to be true" investment program to that vice president's attention.

Roy also began working with an *"Advisor"* trying to figure out how to earn money quickly to pull the company out of its sinkhole. This *"Advisor"* put Roy in touch with a group in Europe working toward acquiring a loan to repay investors and save the company. The *"Advisor"* also discovered additional relevant information about the *"Deceiver"* and connections he had in London.

About that time, another man previously unknown to Roy approached him to give Roy an important revelation. He said he was bringing Roy a "word from God" that would solve all his problems! This *"Prophet"* proceeded to tell of things that no one could have known even as specific as personal matters. And this before any information relative to events had gone public! Obviously, this really got Roy's full attention thinking maybe this was God's way of creating a mighty miracle.

We *knew* it could not possibly be God's will for all the investors to lose their money!

We *knew* it could not possibly be God's will for all these employees to lose their jobs!

We *knew* it could not possibly be God's will for Roy to lose his good reputation!

> *God will supply all my need according to His riches in Christ Jesus*

The *"Prophet"* went on to advise Roy that God wanted him to take this deal to Europe and act as liaison between two groups of people. Further, when this deal was completed Roy would get a "finder's fee," (so to speak) consequently restoring his company, protecting investors, and fulfilling a dream of ministry Roy had been planning for years. It all sounded so good—so scary, but so perfect! God works in mysterious ways, and we knew there's a whole realm of the miraculous that we didn't know much about. And because we were so hungry for a special miracle right then, that we accepted the idea God was working through this stranger to proclaim it to us.

Now knowing that between this new deal from the *"Prophet,"* the loan the *"Advisor"* was putting together, and the additional information about the "*Deceiver*," our faith grew strong—everything was going to be okay.

Unfortunately, a great fear set in and a dark cloud of desperation blurred our logic and common sense. We thought we were full of faith waiting to see how God alone would restore the company, so we quietly pursued each option leading to a solution; but without seeking godly counsel regarding these ventures, we were playing into the hands of Satan. What we really needed was a godly "support team" to share the battle with. But we didn't have one. I should add that we couldn't go to our pastor, because he had money invested in the program that was lost. Had he not been involved we would have turned to him for guidance.

Even with these options before him, Roy lacked the revenue to operate business on a daily basis. He was busy liquidating as many assets as possible to pay back investors. Because interest payments couldn't be paid to investors, public awareness of the issue grew quickly. By October 1985, it was apparent that Roy would have no other choice than file corporate bankruptcy. Even so he strongly promised to do everything possible with the options given him to acquire sufficient funds to return all the money owed to investors.

In January 1986, we packed two suitcases and headed to London to accomplish the missions at hand: First, to complete the loan the "*Advisor*" had put together. Second, to present the deal to the parties involved that the "*Prophet*" brought to us from God, and third to search out this "*Deceiver*" and get the company's money back from him! All this was done with the intent to be back home successfully within three weeks! Wrong! The next six months were spent

I gladly count everything lost in order to know Christ more fully.

chasing things: a loan that didn't happen, two parties who couldn't agree on anything, and a man who was as slippery as an eel. Had our *"Prophet"* really been sent from God, the message he brought for us would have resulted in a resolution for all involved.

We finally realized this so-called prophet was a false prophet with no answers for us. As the weeks went on, we were falling deeper and deeper into the well of deception that Satan had thrown us into. Further, we found out Roy's company was just "small potatoes" compared to some of the other scams the *"Deceiver"* had carried out around the world. We continued to prolong our trip week by week, because the loan the *"Advisor"* was attempting to put together was on again then off again. In hindsight, Satan was leading us on a wild goose chase, but at the time we continued to believe we were being led by God and He would bring us through this for His glory. "He will make this miracle happen; it's His will for the investors to be paid back. He is leading us step-by-step. He will receive all the glory when it's all complete and everything is okay again." We kept telling ourselves these things. But nothing happened. Ultimately the problem was not solved, and we had no other alternatives before us but to go home and face the music. Whatever that was!

Meanwhile back home, while we were off playing detectives for six months in Europe, the man Roy was buying the house from, took back possession of the house along with all our personal belongings: car, clothes, furniture, pictures, life treasures… everything! Because Roy had stopped taking income from his company in September 1985, we were unable to pay him what was owed on the house so he took all our possessions in the house for money owed and not fulfilling our commitment to purchase the house as previously agreed.

At the end of June 1986, Roy and I returned without the loan, without a completed deal, with "some" information on the "*Deceiver*," no home to go to, two suitcases of frequently worn clothes, no money, no jobs, and destroyed reputations. During those six months, the rumors and stories had been in high gear in the local newspapers. "Christian Bible Teacher Bilks Millions in Scam" was the theme of these articles. Even worse, our kids were facing this disgrace every day in school and wondered if we would ever really come home. Although we called them as often as we could, it was difficult to comfort them when they kept hearing so many confusing things. We knew we would go home, but Satan told the world we were hiding out and running from our problems. But we were really trying to run to a solution.

So now what? My dear mom took us into her home not knowing how long it would be before we would be standing on our own again. She was a widow used to living alone. If that wasn't bad enough, she too had lost her investment in the program. On my birthday, August 5, 1986, we sold our wedding rings for $2,500 to pay for legal fees for a $5.6 million personal bankruptcy. From that point on, we literally had to "nickel and dime" our existence between minor jobs here and there plus gifts from friends and our church deacons fund. One-on-one we tried to explain to friends and acquaintances our story and what we had been doing while we were in Europe. Finally, we heard there were federal and state investigations ongoing. We were numb; waiting for the "other shoe to drop."

I am a child of the living God, a joint heir with Christ.

In November 1986, I got a real job with Lincoln Savings, the first bit of stability I had felt for a long time. A friend bought us an old clunker to get around in, and Roy continued to do whatever he could to make money. He tried to sell home security equipment, but his confidence was gone. How do you face the public when you keep remembering what the awful newspaper articles said about you? I remember Roy drove a taxicab all day on Christmas Day. I felt so low I couldn't even think about Christmas. Satan's dark cloud of desperation was wrapped around me so tight that depression choked every breath I would try to take. I was just plain angry with God for letting us down.

Roy was sad and weighed down with the burden he carried for the loss of the investors' money. But his faith remained strong that God was still in control—whatever happened! That was amazing to me because I almost wanted him to be as angry with God as I was—but he wasn't. Roy was so good at trying to encourage me but my anger, bitterness, and confusion were all I could see. I couldn't even seem to cry very much. Just when I didn't think that the pain could get any deeper, on the afternoon of February 4, 1987, Roy got a call from the lawyer that helped us with our personal bankruptcy. There was a warrant out for Roy's arrest and the other shoe dropped! The lawyer had made arrangements for Roy to turn himself in to the authorities the next morning and we had the evening to be with the kids and get ready for the next chapter in the saga.

Roy was held at the Los Angeles County Men's Central Jail with a five-million-dollar bail. Because a bail that high was impossible for us to raise, he stayed incarcerated for six and a half months awaiting trial. If you've never visited someone at county jail, let me paint a picture for you. I would travel into Central Los Angeles to a large gray, cold, dungeon of a building. There I would park my car in a structure with so much graffiti and trash all over that it was hard for me to believe this was a government facility.

I had believed our county would use our tax dollars to keep their properties clean; boy was I wrong! I always visited Roy on Sunday mornings standing in a long line with others waiting to see inmates. I could overhear conversations about the gang fights, drug busts, and robberies, and it all sounded commonplace for them. Most prisoners had been in and out of this horrible place many times. I was wisely instructed before the first visit to "dress down"—wear grubbies, no jewelry, hang on to my purse, and watch my back. Finally, after about one and a half to two and a half hours, I would get to see my sweet, loving husband only to see him behind a glass window and speak through a phone for no more than twenty minutes max! That's not even enough time to get past the initial tears and standard rhetoric of "I'm okay, are you okay? If I know you're okay, then I'll be okay!" But it's all we had for six and one half months, so we made the best of each minute. He could only have one visit a day. Sometimes I'd try to go after work, but it was just too scary for me to drive into that area of town in the old clunker. Yet again, I was experiencing a very different kind of lifestyle!

Roy was arrested with six felony counts against him. But as the preliminary trial ended, the district attorney agreed with Roy's court appointed public defender to drop five counts. The final charge was "selling securities without permission"—regardless of his corporate lawyer's advice that the investment scheme didn't need to be registered. There was no defense and Roy was held responsible because of his company position as chief executive officer. Consequently, Roy pleaded "no contest" with the maximum sentence rendering as many as five years. The sentencing hearing was set for August 5, 1987, again a traumatic event on my birthday!

But the public defender encouraged Roy that since he was a first-time offender, family man, and had already served six and a half months, he figured Roy would get "time served" and be released. Our family showed up and I took a change of clothes for Roy because I was holding on to faith with the expectation he would be released to come home that day. After all, it was my birthday! Instead I was devastated to hear the judge handed down a sentence of four years and remanded to the Chino State Correctional Institution about sixty miles from Mom's house where I was living. I continued to visit Roy in Chino every Sunday. I drove out to the prison to spend the day with him in a rather nice parklike surrounding. During the week, I also had one day off to see him. That was our routine for the next year and a half.

When it came time to be introduced back into society convicts went into a halfway house. And once approved, the last six months of the sentence can be served on a work furlough program. Friends of ours gave Roy a job and he was allowed to work during the day returning to the halfway house at night. Finally, that concluded April 3, 1989 and after twenty-six months of incarceration, Roy was released from the "system" to begin his life again.

Although I only hit the highlights, that was the story portion of my message. I hope you've heard enough to understand how I could have built up a measure of frustration, bitterness, fear, and depression within my heart and mind. As all these events hit me one after another over a three-year period of time. I had no choice but to stay strong and put on a brave front; taking it one day at a time. While Roy was in prison, I obsessively pushed myself working hard and long hours. I even held two jobs for a while. Visiting Roy twice a week - on Sunday and again whatever day off I had during the week; I packed the remaining days so full that I didn't have to stop and feel the pain. I gave myself no time to grieve. If tears started to well up in my eyes, I'd take deep breaths—push the emotion back down inside and tell it, "No, not now! I have no time for you now! I have to keep going. I have no time to think about anything or cry about anything now." I'd shake it off, and soon the emotion would pass. I actually got pretty good at it. Because I knew if I ever let the pain and sadness start coming out, I would lose control and the tears would drown me. I feared I would be unable to regain control if I let it out, even just a little bit. I was afraid I would lose my mind if I let myself freely cry… so I just didn't. Sounds like an easy solution, right? Isn't that what we women do so well anyway? Push it all down deep inside and hope it will just go away?

Since I spent every Sunday with Roy, I wasn't involved in church. So I wasn't getting fed or healing spiritually. I found it very difficult to read my Bible. When I'd tried to read a Psalm it only reminded me of how God rescued His people from pain, yet I was still in agony. I didn't see any rescue for me. I would try to look ahead and plan for the day when we could start over and have a little apartment of our own. I would buy new dishes, towels, and all those things we needed—but even that preparation was painful.

Roy was so good at seeing the big picture of how God would use our experience to help others… but I struggled with that. I couldn't see the vision Roy had, but I kept that to myself. I had blinders around my eyes and all I could see was one day at a time: keep busy, don't lose control, pay the bills, save your money, don't spend money on fun stuff, and that was it! Satan had wrapped his veil of depression over my head and I didn't have the strength to rip it off. No one was close enough to me to really see how deeply depressed I was. After all, I had my act down faultlessly.

During that time, I remember sharing my faith with a coworker speaking of God's great love for us. I truly wanted to help this person come to know Jesus, yet as my witness came out of my mouth, I could hear Jesus in my heart saying; "Oh, Sarah, I love you as much as I love this person and you are closing Me out along with your pain." I recognized I wasn't dealing with all our loss and the tragic events of our recent past. But I just couldn't let go. I had to keep a tight rein on my emotions, because if I lost control… I'd never get it back again.

Almost simultaneously to Roy's release in April 1989, just as we began to rebuild our lives together another major event materialized in my business life. My employer Lincoln Savings was taken over by the government agency regulating the savings and loan industry beginning the now-infamous savings and loan debacle and Charles Keating investigation. If what I had just experienced wasn't bad enough, once again I had to tightly maintain my emotional composure while angry, hurt customers came into the bank yelling at us for stealing their life's investments! During the drama, an elderly customer of my branch took his life because he couldn't see how he could go on without his financial security. But all the while, I had to keep up the unweaving front of strength for both my loyal staff and customers. The whole ordeal was like a replaying nightmare of Roy's company.

On the home front, even though Roy was home, I expected to feel relief and excitement about our future. Instead, the depression I had suppressed for so long rose to the surface with a powerful vengeance. Now within a few short weeks of Roy's return, the tears started pouring out of me and they would not stop! I couldn't push them back like I had previously done. I'd wake up at night with tears running down my cheeks. In the grocery store, tears would come; during holidays and times with the family, the tears would send me into another room to hide. I tried as best as I could to mask it from Roy because I certainly didn't want him to think I wasn't happy he was home. I was truly glad he was there even though I certainly wasn't expressing joy. Somehow the lid of emotional control could no longer be contained compounded by the confusion and the timing of it all. Roy was home, why cry now? The anxiety I felt during the day at work was the hardest to conceal especially compounded with all the confusion and stress at Lincoln Savings. Like before, I would immerse myself in work, but it didn't matter and those heavy tears would overwhelm me at the worst times. Nonetheless I'd always try to find a way to explain it and find my "plastic smiley face" and keep on going!

I could only concentrate for short periods of time before my mind began to wander replaying those old conversations and past situations. I'd mentally rehash all that I could have said or done to have changed the outcome. I wanted to fix everything that happened to make it all better. I was getting confused so easily that the simplest tasks were sometimes just too much for me to handle. The only way I could get through the work day as a bank teller was to tell myself that I had to balance at the end of the shift. As long as I could focus on balancing I didn't have to think about anything else.

Along with the tears and fatigue, came a scary tightness in my chest. And at times, I felt like I couldn't breathe or catch my breath. My heart would be racing so fast, at times I could hear it pounding so loud that I wondered if I was about to have a heart attack! Ultimately though, it was all the months of denying the painful emotion shaking around inside of me and leaking out through my body as stress.

As these ugly feelings came to the surface, they would bring on an intense urge to run away. There were times when I had to leave the room to find a private place to be alone. Some days I wanted to run out the door and not stop until I fainted. Fortunately, I still had enough common sense to realize that was not possible. Subsequently, at work I would regularly go to the restroom or storage room, close the door, huddle into a corner, screaming vigorously in silence, my body trembling with clenched fists. At home I used the small space of our shower stall, closing the door behind me providing a sense of protection from the world while silently screaming as my body shook. I had previously experienced these attacks a few times to a lesser degree, when in Europe and while Roy was in prison. I was able to shake them off then, but actually I was just pushing them down deeper. Although I didn't understand the terms for these frightening emotional bouts at the time, I learned later they were referred to as panic attacks. By this point, I knew I was losing my mind and it scared me because I thought I was having a nervous breakdown and I didn't know what would happen next.

But our Lord God knew what needed to happen next! He used a television commercial to get my attention one evening while home alone. That evening an advertisement for a counseling clinic treating depression and the feelings of suicide mentioned the term "posttraumatic syndrome." Immediately, I linked that definition to what was happening to me. Right in front of me were terms describing disorders experienced after major trauma in our lives and it's just what I had been feeling! It went on to ask ten questions regarding feelings of isolation, confusion, and fear; and number ten asked if I had thoughts of suicide. And finally, "If you can answer 'yes' to even one question, call us today for help. Don't wait!" I had answered yes to nine except for the suicide question. That one I could truly answer "no" primarily because of my daughter. I would never leave her to grow up trying to understand why I took my life. Plus, I knew standing before God; He would replay my life showing how He had planned on bringing us through it all. So suicide was not an option for me, but insanity sure was.

Through this commercial I realized where I was headed, and there was a name attached to it! So I picked up the phone and dialed the number. Someone answered and as I began to stutter my response, just then the call-waiting beeped on my line. I quickly mumbled a good-bye and clicked over to see who distracted me from my call for help. But the line was quiet and after a couple "Hello's", they hung up. Nonetheless that was enough to be my turning point. I really knew then I needed help and finally reached out for it. Returning to the sofa, I prayed with a different request this time. Instead of asking God to take away the pain and tears; I asked Him to help to give whatever was left of me back to Him... one minute at a time. Any bigger time frame than that was not realistic for me. I asked Him to be my counseling clinic. I asked Him to help me remember that I don't ever want to get to question number ten on that list. Again, just the mere knowledge there was a name for the anxiety I was experiencing gave me hope. That was the start of my healing process.

The next morning, I woke up and I still felt the familiar tightness in my chest. Just before I got out of bed I wanted to pray but couldn't speak words. But I remembered the experience the previous evening and I really wanted to get better. At that moment, all I could say was the name of Jesus. I just started my day by saying, "Jesus—Jesus—Jesus."

I said it over and over again, constantly throughout the next days and weeks. While at work I said His name silently and while driving in the car I would shout it out loud. Intellectually, I knew the name of Jesus alone would fight back the demonic depression Satan had wrapped around me. This was the *beginning* of my road back to emotional health, but I didn't have the strength yet to fight Satan off with Scriptures. But I knew I could just call on His name and He would carry me through. With each passing day, when I felt the walls closing in on me again and experiencing urge to "flight," I would make myself focus on saying the name of Jesus. Although the panic attacks didn't disappear immediately, eventually they began to subside. Now each time another attack began to come on me, it became easier to remember the powerful name of Jesus and way down deep inside I could hear His still small voice saying: "Sarah, I love you. You'll get through this. I love you!"

As time went on, these episodes diminished in length and in intensity as my strength to fight Satan with God's Word grew stronger. I realized this depression was a demon, or a spirit of fear that was not from God. In II Timothy 1:7, it told me *"God has not given us (*me*) a spirit of fear, but of power and of love and of a sound mind."* So if God didn't give

> *Everything that belongs to Christ also belongs to me.*

it to me I wasn't going to take it anymore! There's a point in a crisis when, in order to heal, you (yourself) not someone else pulling you along) must crossover to the other side from fear to faith. At that point, you can finally see it as past history and let go of that painful experience so it no longer holds a dominate presence in your daily life.

I began to write short Scriptures or portions of Scriptures on pieces of paper that I called "pocket prayers." Throughout the day, I would take them out and read them to myself. I would also put them in front of me at the teller line and look at them throughout the day. On days when I wore clothes without pockets, I would put them in my shoes. I would tell myself, "I am standing on the Word of God." I would remember short verses and say them to myself over and over until my faith grew strong enough that I could start believing them. An example of one of those verses (my pocket promise) would be, "I can do all things through Christ, who strengthens me."

Let me also say that Roy tried his best to pull me out of my depression. I did my best to hide it as much as possible from him. I didn't want Roy to feel like it was his fault because it wasn't his fault at all. I would tell myself I was protecting him by hiding the truth of my growing emotional problem and how serious it was becoming. But he did know and was praying for me, and he was always there for me!

Healing such feelings manifested as panic attacks, isolation and withdrawal, confusion, and depression requires the expertise of a trained counselor. Even though I desperately needed professional care earlier, it's so comforting to know that the Mighty Counselor, the Prince of Peace, the Great Physician, and the Everlasting Father is always there to meet us right at the place where we are hurting. He does promise in II Corinthians 12:9 (NKJV), "*My grace is sufficient for you, for My strength is made perfect in weakness.*" We are to provide the weakness and He provides the strength. I like that combination!

Psalm 94:19 (NKJV) says, "*In the multitude of my anxieties within me, Your comforts delight my soul.*" No matter what kind of anxieties we face, He has enough comfort for each of them and for all of us. Proverbs 12:25 (NKJV) says, *"Anxiety in the heart of a man (*or woman*) causes depression, but a good word makes it glad."* I could have used a few good words like that during those hurting times. I wonder how it might have been different having a close sister in Christ to walk with me and stand in the gap when I was unable to. Because I chose to drown my sorrow in work and isolation, I didn't have a strong Christian sister in my life to see through my "plastic face" and no other godly woman to challenge me on it or to recognize when another panic attack was likely to strike again. What I needed was a sister in Christ to love and hug me through it. I think if I had been close to a woman who is open and strong and loving in Christ, I would have healed a lot faster.

I am free from all my past sins and failures in Christ.

I know there are some of you who are feeling alone in your personal pain. But you are not alone. The powerful name of Jesus will carry you through anything you are faced with today. And, if you feel so helpless that you're convinced nothing can change or so hopeless you can't survive your situation; then allow the name of Jesus to be your hiding place. In Psalm 32:7 (NKJV) David says to the Lord, *"You are my hiding place. You shall preserve me from trouble. You shall surround me with songs of deliverance."*

You are not alone in what you are facing, and I would venture a guess that there's another woman nearby that has hurt the way you are hurting now. The types of attack Satan deploys don't differ that much between people (health, relationships, family, finances, careers, sin), he just changes the emphasis.

As we learn to become a friend and let someone else be a friend to us; we'll grow to be open, sensitive, and very real with each other because there's a healing touch that Jesus uses when women minister to women. We don't want pity parties or gossip sessions, instead we need a secure place where women can share and find healing with other women. So reach out to someone who needs a listening ear and a hug, and be a sister in Christ who will pray and stand in the gap when the other is hurting. Make yourself available to be that kind of friend and you'll find someone will be there for you when you need it.

As we grow to know each other better as a body of believers, learn how to bond together as a group of women who are committed to making a place of refuge and encouragement for each other and for all women. Finally, let's pray for God's leading and direction for this group as we learn how to reach out to each other.

While Roy was in prison, I lived at Mom's house. Many times during my sleep, I had nightmares about the owner of the house Roy and I had lost. He would be laughing at me and about all the things he had taken away from me. I would awaken feeling disturbed, scared, and remorseful about all the material things now forever lost. I'd remember the furniture Roy and I picked out together. I'd recall my daughter, Michelle's baby pictures, her baby blankie, toys, and dolls that were gone. I'd reminisce about the wedding pictures, high school yearbooks, old family photos that I would never see again. I'd long for the clothes I used to wear to work and feel so good in. I would think back to the Christmas tree filled with ornaments that Michelle and I had made together along with the tree skirt I labored over for so long. Then I'd picture the face of the owner of the house; the one who took it all.

By law he was permitted to take the car and furniture but had a legal obligation to return all our personal items. Because I had no money to contest him in court, this man disregarded the law and our things were gone.

Now I had to somehow let go of them. I did have an address for him, so I wrote him a letter. I needed to tell him that because of Christ, I forgave him. I also asked him to forgive Roy and I for the financial imposition we placed him in. I let it all out on paper. As I reread it over the next few days, the Lord confirmed in my heart that this was right as He helped me to truly believe what I had written. Then I finally stood at the post office and mailed it. Not surprisingly, I never heard anything from him. God had used my writing the letter and the action of putting that letter into the mail box as a tool to cleanse my heart. With that release, I had no more bad dreams about him and the sting of losing those material things was replaced with a peace. That reconciliation spoke to my heart "Everything gets left behind anyway but he can't take away my memories."

There's a story that Roy often tells about a little girl anxiously waiting every day for her daddy to return home from work. Watching for him by the window, she'd run to his arms as he came in the door. Routinely he would sit down in his chair with his loving daughter on his lap as she told him of all the events in her day. She would always say, "Daddy, I love you!" And her Daddy would respond, "I love you too… may I have your necklace?" But this little plastic necklace was her treasure! Because she wouldn't part with it, she answered, "Oh no, Daddy—not my necklace!" Then he would reply, "Okay, honey." Day after day, the little girl eagerly waited for daddy to come home. Regularly she would sit in his lap, hug him then tell him all the fun things she did that day. She so sincerely would say, "Daddy, I love you!" And every day

Daddy would respond, "I love you too... may I have your necklace?" Over and over, the little girl would sadly answer, "Oh no, Daddy, please, not my necklace!" "Okay, honey," he would say. But as the days passed with this daily conversation, the pressure and strain began taking its toll on their relationship. Now the little girl was not as excited to run and jump into his arms anymore. She began holding back, now peeking at him from around the corner consequently both missing out on the sweet times they used to have.

Finally, one evening the little girl came back to her Daddy's big chair and crawled up into his lap crying. "Oh, Daddy, I love you so much! Here, take my necklace!" With that she took off her prized treasure and gave it to her daddy. Silently, he took it and placed it in his pocket then reached into another pocket and pulled out a beautiful, shiny string of genuine pearls for her! "Honey, all I wanted was for you to trust me enough to give me your imitation treasure, so I could replace it with something real and lasting."

As women, we so often hang on to our pain and suffering despite our complaints because we become comfortable with it. The hurt is so close to us that we often talk about letting go, but instead we hold on to it as if it were valuable! Let me encourage you however, to give the Lord your imitation treasures, so that He can replace it with Himself, the Pearl of Great Price. Think about that little girl as you think about what pain you are hanging on to today. Let go! Freely give it to your Heavenly Father, whatever it is, so He can replace it with the lasting beautiful gift of His peace and His presence.

There will never ever be anything that can separate me from God's overwhelming love.

જ ૭

That's "Sarah's Story" told by her, but in my ministry with men I've found many men who have also experienced the anxiety and depression Sarah struggled through. I conducted a survey of over a thousand men who were regular church attendees. Fifty-three percent of these men said that they suffered from loneliness, isolation, or depression. These men live with the pain of fear, worry, and anxiety every day. If you are one of these men, practice making and reading WordPower statements over and over until they become so much a part of you that you begin to believe them and they will eventually help you change your opinion about yourself.

What Sarah called "Pocket Prayers" we now call "*WordPower*" as described in the previous chapter. Following is an exercise that will help you discover the areas in your life for which you need to make WordPower statements.

FORGIVE YOURSELF FOR YOUR NEGATIVES AND PRAISE YOUR POSITIVES

At the end of this chapter you will find a chart with the headings:

"My Negative Acknowledgments" and "My Positive Acknowledgments"

Under "My Negative Acknowledgments," list all the things about you that you consider negative. Under the heading "My Positive Acknowledgments," list all the things that you think are your positive qualities.

After you have completed these lists, take time for prayer. Ask God to forgive you for those negative things in your life whether you consider them sins, failures, weaknesses, or personality faults, etc. Sometimes the most difficult thing is to forgive ourselves. But if God, in all His holiness, is willing to forgive you, the least you can do is forgive yourself. Do as Paul did, *"Brothers, I do not consider that I have made it my own. But one thing I do: forgetting what lies behind and straining forward to what lies ahead, I press on toward the goal for the prize of the upward call of God in Christ Jesus."* (Philippians 3:13–14).

Next, look at the positive qualities you've written about yourself; then thank God for them! Ask God to show you ways to develop each quality to its full potential. Now I'm urging you to sign and date both your positive and negative acknowledgments. This is so you will have a record of the day that you've surrendered those negatives to the Lord and He forgave you for them! Let this date serve also to remind you when you forgave yourself and your commitment date you began developing your positive qualities for His glory.

Look at both lists and find Scriptures that meet the needs expressed on each list and make *WordPower* statements from each Scripture.

In this book, Mentoring His Way, Volume Two, the third Characteristic of a Godly Life, "Being Extremely Valued," reminds us of all that Christ has done for us. Because of Christ, we can accept ourselves as people of extreme value. You should repeat your *WordPower* statements to yourself several times each day.

Negative Acknowledgments / Positive Acknowledgments

Signature	Date	Signature	Date

Notes from My Mentor's Personal Experiences

_____
_____
_____
_____
_____
_____
_____
_____
_____
_____
_____
_____
_____
_____
_____
_____
_____
_____
_____
_____
_____
_____
_____
_____
_____
_____
_____

Scripture Memory Chapter Eight

"Brothers, I do not consider that I have made it my own. But one thing I do: forgetting what lies behind and straining forward to what lies ahead, I press on toward the goal for the prize of the upward call of God in Christ Jesus." (Philippians 3:13)

CHARACTERISTIC FOUR

BEING CHRIST-ACTUALIZED

I AM CHRIST-ACTUALIZED
RATHER THAN SELF-ACTUALIZED

Physical Characteristics of a Godly Life

CHAPTER NINE

FIVE LEVELS OF ASPIRATION

*"I have been crucified with Christ. It is no
longer I who live, but Christ who lives in me.
And the life I now live in the flesh I live by
faith in the Son of God, who loved me and
gave himself for me."* (Galatians 2:20)

The e fourth Personal Characteristic of a Godly Life has
to do with motivation. Motivation is the inner drive in
each of us that keeps us continuously striving toward the
attainment of those goals we have set. Having a godly life
means that we are inspired to become like Christ.

If we fail to set goals, we won't be motivated to be
successful. But if we set goals that are less than what we really
want to achieve or if we set too lofty objectives too far
beyond our capabilities to reach, we will become frustrated
and lose the motivation necessary to be successful. Likewise,
when we allow others to exert a domineering influence over
our goals, we are apt to lose interest. In the event that we run
into obstacles, our motivation declines and it becomes easier
for us to give up. But it's the strength of our desire to reach

our goals is what enables us to stay committed even when we encounter temporary setbacks.

We do things for our own reasons, not other people's reasons. Therefore, your aim must be directed toward those targets significant to you. Achieving your goals have to be so vitally important that you are willing to work and struggle overcoming any barrier that gets in your way. It's critical to realize that your goals take on the greatest significance when they are attributed to a genuine need in your life. Self-motivation and how your drive at reaching goals is affected by your relationship with others; will be discussed in this section.

First, let's explore motivation through the eyes of a prominent secular behavioral scientist to gain insight of the world's theories on what prompts us to strive for various levels of success and fulfillment. Are these concepts applicable and are they accurate? Or do they limit us in attaining our highest aspirations? Are they in agreement or conflict with God's plan for our lives? Next, we will look at God's plan for a successful life. We will learn what God says about motivation through trusting in Him, His Word, and His promises, putting our faith in Him, having faith in ourselves consequently enabling us to have the confidence in reaching our goals then having those goals bear fruit.

By the world's standards, we are either a success or a failure. But God's method can be found in our hearts. Once we are standing on the solid foundation of Christ, He measures our victory by how we walk in the Spirit and daily conforming to the image of His Son. But anything built in our flesh while conforming to this world suffers loss.

I walk in the Spirit not in the flesh.

> *"According to the grace of God given to me, like a skilled master builder I laid a foundation, and someone else is building upon it. Let each one take care how he builds upon it. For no one can lay a foundation other than that which is laid, which is Jesus Christ. Now if anyone builds on the foundation with gold, silver, precious stones, wood, hay, straw— each one's work will become manifest, for the Day will disclose it, because it will be revealed by fire, and the fire will test what sort of work each one has done. If the work that anyone has built on the foundation survives, he will receive a reward. If anyone's work is burned up, he will suffer loss, though he himself will be saved, but only as through fire"* (I Corinthians 3:10–15).

To gain motivation as we develop into all God wants us to be, it is important that we know ourselves and what our needs are. Therefore, it's essential to know the level of your needs and what importance they will have on your motivation in setting goals necessary to meet those needs.

MASLOW'S LEVELS OF ASPIRATION

My forty plus years in the business world taught me that most workplace motivation is based on humanistic incentive. So let's take a look at some of these specific worldly principles so that we can compare them to what God's Word has to say.

In his book, *The Dynamic Review in Motivation*, behavioral scientist, A. H. Maslow defined five categories of human motivation with each level of aspiration classified by rank. Now let's look at each level carefully one by one to understand what is involved. Maslow says that we begin at the first level and progress toward the fifth level as we mature. Although it's possible God has revealed to Maslow truths about human motivation and how it works, Maslow doesn't give God credit for this discovery. Nevertheless, the following are his five levels of aspiration:

FIRST LEVEL – PHYSICAL
(Food, drink, sex, warmth, sleep, things we can touch and feel)
A person at the first level is primarily concerned with obtaining the basic necessities to sustain life, maintain a comfortable environment and find physical gratification.

SECOND LEVEL – SAFETY
(Feeling of security, free from pain, free from worry, familiar with surroundings and ideas)
The person who finds himself on the second level is usually motivated by fear of loss. They are afraid of change and caught up in worry and insecurities often anxious if they're able to earn enough just to maintain for today. They're focused on economic factors and the protection of their job and assets for the future.

THIRD LEVEL – LOVE

(The need to feel loved, rewarding personal relationships, secure friendships, a feeling of belonging, approval, and acceptance)

Characterized in third level, a person wants to feel loved, needed, and appreciated by others. They seek—even strive—for social recognition. They desire to be an important part of a team, and to be assured their contributions are meaningful. They fear rejection and criticism.

> *God's perfect love has cast out all my fears.*

FOURTH LEVEL – SELF ESTEEM

(Self-respect, self-worth, feelings of adequacy, prestige, confidence, recognition, appreciation, and importance)

A person existing primarily on the fourth level is concerned more about self-image and less inclined to worry about what others think. This person's fulfillment is realized when the goals set for themselves are achieved to their personal satisfaction. They seek self-confidence, pushing to fine-tune their own talents and abilities. Self-criticism becomes more a factor in an effort to improve and prove themselves rather than a concern for being accepted by others.

FIFTH LEVEL – SELF ACTUALIZATION

(Feeling of achievement, growth, realization of reaching one's full potential or capacity, a challenge, or opportunity)

A person arriving at the fifth level of aspiration knows what they want out of life while understanding they are fully capable of getting it.

They use their full potential in every facet of life completely comfortable in themselves. This individual's self-image is secure having the unsolicited respect and admiration of others. They are continuously seeking new challenges that test their maximum abilities enabling them to reach greater heights in growth and achievement. They're not afraid of change; instead, thrive on it.

HOW DO YOU KNOW WHAT LEVEL YOU'RE ON?

As we develop an understanding of each of these levels, you may discover you have some unsatisfied needs at each level. Therefore, it's important to determine which level is predominant in your life. The level at which you are expending the most effort to succeed is your dominant level. This is the level where you are now. This is the area of your life that you are the most concerned about and that is the most important to you.

According to Maslow, these levels are designed in us to be progressive in nature—they're not meant to stagnate. And throughout my experience training thousands of people in North America over the last five decades, I have found that when a person stops growing spiritually, personally and professionally; they begin digressing. They don't remain stagnant. Too often we stumble over failures in our lives when we don't grasp then use the potential that God has given us to its fullest.

So here is where the motivation factor comes in: If we want to grow we can! If there's a desire to change and aspire to greater heights—we can! We must first develop a burning desire to move ahead. But desire though, in and by itself, isn't enough. Left alone to stand like a flickering candle in the wind, it will eventually die.

God helps me to do what honors Him the

200

To succeed desire requires action, so before we act we must motivate ourselves to do so. Desires without actions are dreams without substance. Motivation is the substance that can turn our dreams into reality.

THREE PERSONALITY TYPES

People behave in certain ways for one of three reasons:

1. To gain reward
2. To avoid punishment
3. To receive acceptance

We are motivated to fulfill our levels of aspiration through a principle known as "cause and effect." This principle describes the effect self-confidence, fear, and acceptance impact the way we act instilling in us a "fear-oriented," an "acceptance-oriented," or a "self-confidence-oriented" personality.

Well-known motivational guru Tony Robins has developed an entire message around two of these personality groups: people motivated to avoid pain or those motivated to receive pleasure. Though his work encompasses much more, he's built a financial empire primarily on teaching these two principles.

THE FEAR ORIENTED PERSONALITY

Some factors that cause a fear-oriented personality are the disapproval of parents, a strict home life, punishment for small misdeeds, taboos constantly pointed out in childhood, and past failures in school and on the job.

The individual with a fearful personality has become much more concerned with avoiding punishment than in gaining rewards. They are fearful of failure or embarrassment. Both avoid any action that might result in a rejection, dismissal, scolding, humiliation, or a penalty. They routinely tend to resist change and new ideas, desiring instead to maintain the status quo. They have a fear of failure and are full of worry and doubt often thinking in terms of the worst-case scenario. They seek to please because they can't stand to be the object of displeasure. Their only motivation to succeed is the ramifications of what failure will have on their life. They are materialistic and fears any type of loss that might affect their security. They avoid adversity, change, and challenges in the workplace and is content with sameness to avoid rocking the boat.

The fearful personality seeks to avoid punishment or loss. They avoid punishment primarily to satisfying their basic needs. Their motivation is affected by the first two levels of aspiration as put forth by Maslow: physical or safety.

THE ACCEPTANCE ORIENTED PERSONALITY

The major factors leading to an acceptance-oriented personality include the approval and acceptance of others. The feeling of being loved by—and belonging to—a peer group is of utmost importance to his well-being and self-image.

The individual with an acceptance personality seeks reward, especially the approval of others, and is even willing to take risks obtaining their endorsement. But they won't risk the disapproval of others. Such an individual's rewards center specifically on the loving acceptance of a small group of friends close enough to really understand them.

They tend to thrive in an environment providing a feeling of acceptance and belonging. Their motivation is primarily on Maslow's third level of aspiration—love. These are team players who look to other group members to recognize their contributions and be rewarded accordingly. Acceptance-driven individuals strive for success motivated by "that-a-boys" and "kudos" for a job well done.

THE SELF-CONFIDENT ORIENTED PERSONALITY

Contributing factors leading to a self-confident personality involve positive inputs received from others throughout life. Self-confident individuals were rewarded by their parents when they did well in school. They were rewarded by employers for their continuous outstanding job performance. Even their families provide rewards for success including their spouse and children's material well-being. The self-confident strive for each new success to gain rewards until the level of self-actualization has been reached.

The individual with a self-confident personality is more concerned with gaining rewards than avoiding loss. This person is strongly reward-oriented, and the rewards sought primarily are those suggested in Maslow's fourth and fifth levels of aspiration: self-esteem and self-actualization.

The self-confident individual is motivated by his attitude toward himself. They are driven to become "number one," reaching the highest pinnacle, and putting their skills and abilities to the test. The image they have of themselves becomes an aura of confidence and respect. A self-confident individual will climb a mountain for self-fulfillment, not for the gratification of others. They accomplish their goals because they know they can. They revel in change looking forward to adversity, and disdains the status quo considering it a setback to growth.

Do you see yourself in any of these three personality types? As I mentioned earlier, each of us may have some combination of all these attributes. Which one is most predominant in you?

MOTIVATIONAL TYPES LINKED WITH THE PERSONALITY TYPES

There are three kinds of motivation that are usually associated with the three personality types described above: Fear, Incentive, and Attitude.

Fear Motivation

Our self-image has been greatly affected by the type of motivation others used on us as a child. I remember growing up in fourteen foster homes. Although many of my foster parents were wonderful people, some were frighteningly mean. As a small child, I wet the bed. I remember one particularly cruel foster parent would threaten me continuously about it. So whenever I did it he would rub my bare bottom in the snow. Many nights I would try my best not to fall asleep so that I wouldn't have an accident but no matter how hard I tried I would always fail. Early the next morning, he would come to my bedroom only to find me lying in a wet puddle again. Then this abusive bully would rip my pants off and drag me out into the snow and rub my bottom in the snow until it would bleed. All the while saying things such as, "Why God would allow such a useless piece of crap (my word) to exist is beyond me. You are the most stupid, weak little sissy I have ever known." I thought... *"even God must think I'm useless and stupid."*

We need to be extremely careful of the things we say to our children! A child's opinion of themselves is often formed as a direct result of what parents convey. I've heard dads say things like, "You're an idiot!" or "You're too stupid to know what day it is" or "You'll never learn." Comments like: "You're just not smart enough," "You're such a loser," or "You'll never succeed at anything" serve only to diminish and condemn. The psalmist said of God, *"Your eyes saw my unformed substance; in your book were written, every one of them, the days that were formed for me, when as yet there was none of them"* (Psalm 139:16). God has a plan for each of His children, and He warns us not to interfere with His plan. *"But whoever causes one of these little ones who believe in me to sin, it would be better for him to have a great millstone fastened around his neck and to be drowned in the depth of the sea"* (Matthew 18:6).

Remember that the threat of punishment or fear of loss used over and over forms a root of insecurity in a child. Fear motivation could negatively affect them for the rest of their lives. Therefore, even though at times when it may appear necessary, don't use fear to motivate your children! Provoking your child with fear merely yields temporary results and eventually turns them against you.

Employers who use fear to motivate their employees to perform intimidate them with negativity including loss of pay, and even the security of their jobs. Sometimes it's the threat of loss of promotion or a bonus that's used. Why? Because many business owners and managers are themselves haunted with the fear of failure! Since they live with fear of loss, it is natural to use this method of motivation on others.

Unfortunately, employees eventually quit, become passive, or unmotivated. Either way, we see that fear motivation is temporary.

Incentive Motivation

Incentives are rewards for performance. Parents may use incentives to get their kids to clean their rooms, to do homework, or chores around the house. This is a much-better motivation than fear. The shortcoming of incentives, however, is the prize must keep getting bigger with each new task. Soon the reward gets so big that we price ourselves out of the game. We'll end up promising a new sports car for graduating from high school! Additionally, as soon as the prize is received the enthusiasm stops until the next new enticement is agreed upon. Subsequently, as good as an incentive motivation seems to be, it is also temporary in nature.

In a previous role as national sales manager within a large financial corporation, we would put on an annual sales contest to motivate our sales force typically during our slower business months in October through February. The prize would change every year: One year it would be a trip to Hawaii, the next would have to be even better—like a cruise in the Caribbean. Unfortunately, as soon as the contest was over business came to a standstill and it took two to three months to get production back to normal. Therefore, Incentive Motivation—like fear motivation—is temporary and external.

Attitude Motivation

Attitude motivation is internal motivation. It is a means of helping us change our attitude about ourselves. The

Bible uses similar terms such as, "Renew your mind" or "as a man thinks in his heart, so is he." *I am straining to win the race and receive the prize.* Attitude motivation is a way to renew our mind ensuring what we think about ourselves is positive. Remember my high school principal Mr. Adkins? He used attitude motivation as he kept constantly refreshing my thoughts "that I could be anything I wanted to be" or "do anything I wanted to do." After hearing it over and over, I began to believe it. Once I believed it, I started acting on it. Eventually, I developed a self-confidence that helped me accomplish much more in life than I could have imagined before.

Positive affirmation is repeating positive thoughts over and over to ourselves. As we say words like "I can do it," we begin programming these positive attitudes into our minds until we begin to believe them. After we believe them, we begin to act on them. Attitude motivation is telling yourself that you can accomplish anything you choose to do. It's the ice cubes we talked about in changing the big bucket of hot black coffee into cold clear water. It is reminding us of our good qualities. Attitude motivation is capable of creating permanent change from the inside. Feeding in the right thoughts will eventually help us to achieve self-actualization.

We have briefly discussed what motivates us to set goals seeking gratification solely to satisfy our needs. But in the next three chapters, we'll discover the transformation in our lives by applying God's Word through WordPower in fulfilling each level of aspiration. As Christians go beyond self-actualization to become Christ-actualized there are limitless possibilities becoming all God desires for us to become.

We have discussed motivation from the humanistic world view. Now we will examine motivation in light of the Scriptures by examining each of the levels of aspiration demonstrating how they are fulfilled in Christ. Because as Christians, we don't have to rely on the world's methods of motivation. Love should always be our motivation.

I am the righteousness of God in Christ Jesus.

Chapter Nine

FIVE LEVELS OF ASPIRATION

Questions for home study and group discussions

List the five "Levels of Aspiration."

What level(s) of aspiration is the "Fearful" personality on? Explain.

What level(s) of aspiration is the "Acceptance" personality on?   Explain.

What level(s) of aspiration is the "Self-Confident" personality on?   Explain.

What level do you primarily see yourself on?

Notes from My Mentor's Personal Experiences

_____
_____
_____
_____
_____
_____
_____
_____
_____
_____
_____
_____
_____
_____
_____
_____
_____
_____
_____
_____
_____
_____
_____
_____
_____
_____
_____

Scripture Memory Chapter Nine

"I have been crucified with Christ. It is no longer I who live, but Christ who lives in me. And the life I now live in the flesh I live by faith in the Son of God, who loved me and gave himself for me." (Galatians 2:20)

CHAPTER TEN

FULFILLING PHYSICAL
AND SAFETY NEEDS

"And my God will supply every need of yours according to his riches in glory in Christ Jesus." (Philippians 4:19)

Here we'll discuss how Christ will satisfy our physical and safety needs as earlier described by Maslow. We have learned from the world that Mr./Ms. Fearful is motivated by fear of loss. In contrast, the Bible tells us as followers of Christ, we don't need to worry about the basic needs of life because God has promised to supply them for us.

One of the most effective methods of fulfilling our physical and safety needs is to develop WordPower statements from the Scriptures. For example, below are several verses that describe God's promises. At the end of the paragraph explaining the verse, I have written some suggested WordPower statements.

FEAR DOES NOT COME FROM GOD

"For God gave us a spirit not of fear but of power and love and self-control" (II Timothy 1:7). When a Christian finds himself fearing possible loss, he needs to realize that fear is not coming from God. As previously stated, fear is a spirit placed on us by our enemy. Satan will try to frighten us into doubting God's provisions. So when distress and anxiety hits you, use your authority in the name of Jesus to end Satan's influence on you. Because fear cannot harm you, use the authority given in Jesus's name to stop Satan and his demons. Surrender that worry to the Holy Spirit. If need be, go back and study Spiritual Characteristic Three in Mentoring His Way Volume 1.

> *God did not give me a spirit of fear; fear comes from the enemy.*

- God has not given me a spirit of fear.
- I have Christ's authority over all the power of the enemy.
- God's perfect love casts out my fear.
- I have a sound mind; I do not fear.

DON'T BE ANXIOUS ABOUT ANYTHING

God has promised that He will provide everything we need. So we must learn to trust God to do what He says He will do.

"Therefore, I tell you, do not be anxious about your life, what you will eat or what you will drink, nor

> *I am not worried or anxious about anything.*

212

about your body, what you will put on. Is not life more than food, and the body more than clothing? Look at the birds of the air: they neither sow nor reap nor gather into barns, and yet your heavenly Father feeds them. Are you not of more value than they? And which of you by being anxious can add a single hour to his span of life? And why are you anxious about clothing? Consider the lilies of the field, how they grow: they neither toil nor spin yet I tell you even Solomon in all his glory was not arrayed like one of these. But if God so clothes the grass of the field, which today is alive and tomorrow is thrown into the oven, will he not much more clothe you, O you of little faith? Therefore, do not be anxious, saying, 'What shall we eat?' or 'What shall we drink?' or 'What shall we wear?' For the Gentiles seek after all these things, and your heavenly Father knows that you need them all. But seek first the kingdom of God and his righteousness, and all these things will be added to you. "Therefore, do not be anxious about tomorrow, for tomorrow will be anxious for itself. Sufficient for the day is its own trouble" (Matthew 6:25–34)

We must learn to accept by faith that God wants us to have a prosperous life, trusting in Him to be our provider. Never doubt for a moment His ability to get the job done by following the direction of the Holy Spirit as He guides us toward the fulfillment of our needs. There is no need for anxiety to overwhelm us. He leads—we follow. By following Him, we reap bountiful harvests that He has promised us.

By maturing in our walk with Christ, we are learning through His Word to sow first in faith and then we'll begin to reap the rewards He has promised. As we trust in Him all fear and doubt dispel from our lives

My Heavenly Father knows perfectly well what I need.

and we begin realizing our full God-given potential to succeed. God does His part, and then we do our part through the Holy Spirit. His blessings are unlimited.

- I don't worry about anything.
- Worry does not add one moment to my life.
- My Heavenly Father knows perfectly well what I need.
- God provides my needs. I have given Him first place in my heart.
- I trust and obey God in everything.
- I am not anxious about anything.
- I trust God to take care of my tomorrows.
- I live one day at a time.

CHRIST IS OUR SHEPHERD

The Bible tells us that Christ cares for us the way a shepherd takes care of his sheep. In John, chapter 10, Jesus is called the Good Shepherd who cares for His sheep. We find another picture of our Lord as shepherd in Psalm 23:

"The LORD is my shepherd; I shall not want. He makes me lie down in green pastures. He leads me beside still waters. He restores my soul. He leads me in paths of righteousness for his name's sake. "Even though I walk through the valley of the shadow of death, I will fear no evil, for you are with me; your rod and your staff, they comfort me. You prepare a table before me in the presence of my enemies; you anoint my head with oil; my cup overflows. Surely goodness and mercy shall follow me all the days of my life, and I shall dwell in the house of the LORD forever" (Psalm 23:1–6).

I trust God to take care of my tomorrows also.

Let's look at some WordPower statements from Psalm 23

- I have everything I need.
- God restores my failing health.
- God helps me do what honors Him the most.
- No matter what happens I will not be afraid.
- God is within me, guarding, guiding all the way.
- My blessings overflow.
- His unfailing kindness shall be with me all the days of my life.

GOD WILL SUPPLY ALL YOUR NEED

"And my God will supply every need of yours according to his riches in glory in Christ Jesus" (Philippians 4:19). Paul says that God will supply all our needs. He does this according to His riches in glory by Christ Jesus. If this is true, why should I worry about anything? The only possible reason

God is within me guarding, guiding all the way.

I would have to worry is disbelief. But if I do not believe that God will do what He says He will do, and then I am calling God a liar.

As Christians to worry about whether our needs will be met, is to tell God that we don't trust Him and we do not believe His Word. That's why I'd encourage you to write the verse above into *WordPower* statements and read them aloud over and over until we begin to believe God's promise and accept the fact that this applies to us.

Here is a suggestion for writing this promise into *WordPower* statements.

- Father, I trust you to supply all my needs according to your riches.
- I do not worry about my needs.
- I trust you completely to do what you said you would do.

GOD WILL KEEP YOU SAFE FROM ALL HARM

Throughout King David's life from before he ascended to the throne and was pursued by Saul until deposed by his son Absalom, his life was constantly in danger. But he never doubted that God would protect him. He knew that God would bring him safely through every situation. In the book of Psalms, David attributes his confidence in God's protection.

The Lord will work out His plans for my life. | *"For the righteous will never be moved; he will be remembered forever. He is not afraid of bad news; his heart is firm, trusting in the* LORD. *His heart is steady; he will not be afraid, until he looks in triumph on his adversaries"* (Psalm 112:6–8).

Here's some *WordPower* statements from Psalm 112:6-8

- I will not be overthrown by any circumstances.
- I do not fear bad news, nor do I live in dread of what might happen.
- I have settled in my mind that God will take care of me.
- That is why I am not afraid but can calmly face my problems.
- God's constant care of me makes a deep impression on all who see it.

> *"Though I walk in the midst of trouble, you preserve my life; you stretch out your hand against the wrath of my enemies, and your right hand delivers me. The LORD will fulfill his purpose for me your steadfast love, O LORD, endures forever. Do not forsake the work of your hands"* (Psalm 138:7–8).

Here's some WordPower statements from Psalm 138:7-8

- God will bring me safely through all my troubles.
- Lord, your power will save me.
- The Lord will work out His purpose for my life.
- Lord, your loving kindness toward me will continue forever.

Paul tells us,

> *"Through Him also we have [our] access (entrance, introduction) by faith into this grace (state of God's favor) in which we [firmly and safely] stand. And let us rejoice and exult in our hope of experiencing and enjoying*

My character produces the habit of joyful and confident hope.

the glory of God. Moreover [let me also be full of joy now!] let us exult and triumph in our troubles and rejoice in our sufferings, knowing that pressure and affliction and hardship produce patient and unswerving endurance. And endurance (fortitude) develops maturity of character (approved faith and tried integrity). And character [of this sort] produces [the habit of joyful and confident hope] of eternal salvation" (Romans 5:2–4, AMP).

Here's some *WordPower* statements from Romans 5:2-4

- Through Christ I have access by faith into God's grace.
- I firmly and safely stand in God's grace.
- I rejoice and exult in my experiencing and enjoying the glory of God.
- God the Father fills me with His joy.
- I exult and triumph in my troubles and rejoice in my suffering.
- I know that pressure, affliction, and hardship produce patience.
- Endurance develops my character, which gives me approved faith.
- My character produces the habit of joyful and confident hope.

Once these truths are hidden deep in our hearts, we'll be able to accept that God has fulfilled all our physical and safety needs. Then we can move on to experience how God's love will fulfill all our "love" needs, as Maslow discusses in his third level of aspiration.

Chapter Ten

FULFILLING PHYSICAL
AND SAFETY NEEDS

Questions for home study and group discussions

How do we know that we don't have to live in fear?
II Timothy 1:7

How do we overcome worry and anxiety?
Matthew 6:25–34

What promises does God give us in Psalm 23:1–6 concerning
our security?

What is God's promise concerning supplying our needs?
Philippians 4:19

How do we know that God will keep us safe?
Psalms 112:6–8; 138:7–8

Physical Characteristics of a Godly Life

Notes from My Mentor's Personal Experiences

_____
_____
_____
_____
_____
_____
_____
_____
_____
_____
_____
_____
_____
_____
_____
_____
_____
_____
_____
_____
_____
_____
_____
_____

Scripture Memory Chapter Ten

"And my God will supply every need of yours according to his riches in glory in Christ Jesus." (Philippians 4:19)

CHAPTER ELEVEN

FULFILLING LOVE NEEDS

"There is no fear in love, but perfect love
casts out fear." (I John 4:18a)

GOD IS THE SOURCE OF ALL LOVE

As we explored earlier, Mr./Ms. Acceptance is motivated by the need for acceptance and recognition. They need to know and be constantly reassured that they are loved, accepted, and have a sense of belonging. Throughout this book we have made numerous references to God's love. Even though it may seem a bit repetitious to go over these same verses, it helps us realize that God has met all our love needs in Christ. Therefore, I've purposefully repeated them over again until we're able to accept them as truth. Although we'll share some of them again here, please go back and reread the chapters on "Love Motivated" and "Extremely Valued." Remember always, true love is from God because God is love (agape).

God showed His great love for me by sending Jesus Christ.

GOD HAS ACCEPTED YOU INTO HIS FAMILY AND YOU BELONG!

God has looked down from His most Holy Place in heaven once seeing you in all your sin but has shown how very much He loves you by accepting you just as you are with all your iniquities, weaknesses, and failures. Now you are a child of the King and joint heir with Christ. So He knows who you are and what you've been like. But you don't have to be perfect to please God. That's because Jesus paid the penalty for your sin and made things right through Christ's blood redeeming you from every transgression in your entire life!

"But God shows his love for us in that while we were still sinners, Christ died for us. Since, therefore, we have now been justified by his blood, much more shall we be saved by him from the wrath of God. For if while we were enemies we were reconciled to God by the death of his Son, much more, now that we are reconciled, shall we be saved by his life. More than that, we also rejoice in God through our Lord Jesus Christ, through whom we have now received reconciliation" (Romans 5:8–11).

I am able to hold my head high no matter what happens.

God has declared you not guilty! You do not stand in judgment before God. You are forgiven of all your past failures and sins. God does not hold any of them against you. What blessings He must have for us now that we are His friends.

God is your friend. You have been accepted. You belong to the family.

- God showed His great love for me by sending Christ.
- How much more will He do for me now that He has declared me not guilty?
- Christ has saved me from all God's wrath to come.
- What blessings God has for me now that I am His friend.
- The Triune God lives within me.
- I rejoice in my wonderful relationship with God.

> *"And hope does not put us to shame, because God's love has been poured into our hearts through the Holy Spirit who has been given to us"* (Romans 5:5).

- I am able to hold my head high no matter what happens.
- I know how dearly God loves me.
- I feel God's warm love everywhere within me.
- God has given me His Holy Spirit to fill my heart with His love.

"For you did not receive the spirit of slavery to fall back into fear, but you have received the Spirit of adoption as sons, by whom we cry, "Abba! Father!" The Spirit himself bears witness with our spirit that we are children of God,

I do not act like a cringing fearful slave. I behave like God's very own child.

and if children, then heirs—heirs of God and fellow heirs with Christ, provided we suffer with him in order that we may also be glorified with him" (Romans 8:15–17).

- I did not receive the bondage again to fear.
- I behave like God's very own child; I call Him, Abba, Father.
- The Holy Spirit speaks to me deep in my heart.
- The Holy Spirit tells me that I really am God's child.
- Since I am God's child I will share in His treasures.
- All God gives to His Son Jesus is now mine too.
- I share in Christ's suffering not just in His glory.

NOTHING CAN SEPARATE US FROM THE LOVE OF GOD

God's Word declares over and over that He loves us. But it's also critically important we understand we can never be separated from God's love. God's love is permanent, eternal, and unconditional.

All the power of hell cannot keep God's love from me.

"For I am sure that neither death nor life, nor angels nor rulers, nor things present nor things to come, nor powers, nor height nor depth, nor anything else in all creation, will be able to separate us from the love of God in Christ Jesus our Lord" (Romans 8:38–39).

- No matter where I go or what I do, nothing can ever separate me from God's love.
- All the power of hell itself cannot keep God's love from me.
- My fears or my worries will not keep God's love from me.

FOR ACCEPTANCE AND BELONGING GET INVOLVED WITH A CHURCH

The Bible tells us that if we truly belong to Christ then our lives will demonstrate that by the way we love others, especially Christians. It's very important to understand our deep-rooted need to belong. Let me urge you then to get involved in a congregation where the love of God is expressed among its fellowship of believers. There, your need for acceptance and belonging will be quickly satisfied. Learn God's principle of giving first like Jesus was given. Begin by finding a church where you can give your love to others and soon your need to be loved will be met. Remember in John 13:34 it says, *"A new commandment I give to you, that you love one another: just as I have loved you, you also are to love one another."*

- We show our love for God by showing our love for others.

"Beloved, let us love one another, for love is from God, and whoever loves has been born of God and knows God. Anyone who does not love does not know God, because God is love. In this the love of God was made

Since God loves me so much it causes me to love others too.

manifest among us, that God sent his only Son into the world, so that we might live through him. In this is love, not that we have loved God but that he loved us and sent his Son to be the propitiation for our sins. Beloved, if God so loved us, we also ought to love one another. No one has ever seen God; if we love one another, God abides in us and his love is perfected in us" (I John 4:7–12).

- I practice loving others, for my love comes from God.
- Because I am a child of God, I show love and kindness to others.
- My love for others is growing as I know God better—God is love.
- It is not my love for God, but His love for me.
- Since God loved me as much as that, I love others too.
- My love shows that God lives in me.
- God's love within me grows even stronger.

> *"If anyone says, 'I love God,' and hates his brother, he is a liar; for he who does not love his brother whom he has seen cannot love God whom he has not seen. And this commandment we have from him: whoever loves God must also love his brother."* (I John 4:20–21).

- Because I love God, I also love my brothers in Christ.

- Even though I have never seen God, I love Him.
- I love not only God, but my brother also.

God has said that we are to express our love for Him by loving the brethren. So it makes sense that finding a church where you can have fellowship with other Christians will help you gain acceptance and fulfill your need for belonging.

LOVE GROWS MORE PERFECT AND COMPLETE IN CHRIST

"There is no fear in love, but perfect love casts out fear. For fear has to do with punishment, and whoever fears has not been perfected in love. We love because he first loved us." (I John 4:18–19).

God's perfect love eliminates all my fears.

- I need have no fear of God because He loves me perfectly.
- His perfect love eliminates all my fears.
- I am never afraid of what God might do to me.
- I am fully convinced that God really loves me.
- My love for God comes from Him loving me first.

God meets our need for love, acceptance, and belonging in Christ and His Church. Now as we grow in intimacy with God and in our desire to conform to Christ's image, we no longer feel unloved or unaccepted. Now we can move on to the next step on Maslow's Levels of Aspiration: self-esteem and self-actualization.

In summary, we have seen how to eliminate worry and fear in our lives by living daily in God's Word. We have learned how God's love provides for us, filling our hearts with his love, enabling us to love Him and others in return. Finally, we have discovered a wonderful sense of belonging.

I am fully convinced that God truly loves me.

Now that our physical and love needs are met, we're now ready to take the final step to a higher level. So let's continue in God's Word as He shows us how to reach our fullest potential by magnifying and glorifying Him through His Son, Christ Jesus.

Chapter Eleven

FULFILLING LOVE NEEDS

Questions for home study and group discussion

How do we get God's love?   Romans 5:5

How did God prove His love for us?   Romans 5:8

What is the result of being God's very own child?
Romans 8:15–17

What can separate us from the love of God?
Romans 8:38–39

What does God's perfect love do for us?   I John 4:18

Notes from My Mentor's Personal Experiences

_____

_____

_____

_____

_____

_____

_____

_____

_____

_____

_____

_____

_____

_____

_____

_____

_____

_____

_____

_____

_____

_____

_____

_____

_____

Scripture Memory **Chapter Eleven**

"There is no fear in love, but perfect love casts out fear." (I John 4:18a)

CHAPTER TWELVE

FULFILLING SELF ESTEEM AND SELF ACTUALIZATION NEEDS

"I can do all things through him who strengthens me." (Philippians 4:13)

Returning to our example of the Self-Confident individual, we recall they are motivated by the need to gain reward through self-achievement. They desire to be the best at each area of their life. The Self-Confident person works hard at developing and maintaining a positive attitude and attempt to be the best in every facet of life. They have accepted their self as a person of value and hold to a keen awareness of self-worth and self-love. Jesus said that we must love others as much as we love ourselves. Mr./Ms. Self-Confident are able to love others because they no longer struggle with predominate feelings of low self-esteem.

This individual is now able to concentrate on helping to fulfill the needs of others without needing personal attention. Mr. Self-Confident is also becoming self-actualized by developing his full potential. He is motivated by the desire to be the best he can be, for his own personal satisfaction.

Self-actualization is now the continuing goal of his life. The Apostle Paul is an example of a person who was self-actualized.

He said, *"Be imitators of me, as I am of Christ."* (I Corinthians 11:1)

Paul knew that he was doing the best he could to live the way he believed God wanted him to live. So he was able to tell others to follow his example in order to assure that they too would be living the right way. Paul believed that he could do anything he wanted to because **Others imitate me, just as I also imitate Christ.** he knew where the source of his strength came from.

"I can do all things through Christ who strengthens me" (Philippians 4:13).

- Imitate me, just as I also imitate Christ.
- I can do all things through Christ who strengthens me.

I can do all things through Christ who strengthens me. Paul continued to develop his full potential by striving to be the best at whatever he believed God wanted him to achieve. He saw life as a race and a challenge. According to Paul, life was to be lived to its fullest to the glory of God. He desired the reward that only God could give him. He used Jesus as an example of perseverance.

"Therefore, since we are surrounded by so great a cloud of witnesses, let us also lay aside every weight, and sin which clings so closely, and let us run with endurance the

> *race that is set before us, looking to Jesus,*
> *the founder and perfecter of our faith, who*
> *for the joy that was set before him endured*
> *the cross, despising the shame, and is seated*
> *at the right hand of the throne of God"*
> (Hebrews 12:1–2).

- There is a huge crowd of men watching me from the grandstands.
- I have stripped off every sin that has slowed me down.
- I have gotten rid of those sins that wrap themselves around my feet.
- I run with patience the race that God has set before me.
- I keep my eyes on Jesus, my leader and instructor.
- I am willing to die a shameful death for the joy of serving Christ.

> *"That I may know him and the power of his*
> *resurrection, and may share his sufferings,*
> *becoming like him in his death, that by any*
> *means possible I may attain the resurrection*
> *from the dead. Not that I have already*
> *obtained this or am already perfect, but I press*
> *on to make it my own, because*
> *Christ Jesus has made me his*
> *own. Brothers, I do not consider*
> *that I have made it my own. But*
> *one thing I do: forgetting what lies*
> *behind and straining forward to*
> *what lies ahead, I press on toward*
> *the goal for the prize of the*
> *upward call of God in Christ Jesus"*
> (Philippians 3:10–14).

I keep my eyes on Jesus my leader and instructor.

- I have given up everything; it is the only way to know Christ.
- I want to know what it means to suffer and die with Christ.
- I am one of those who lives in the fresh newness of life.
- I work for that day when I will be all that Christ saved me to be.
- I am bringing all my energies to bear on this one thing.
- I have forgotten the past and am looking forward to what lies ahead.
- I strain to reach the end of the race and receive the prize.
- God is calling me to Heaven because of what Christ Jesus did for me.

Paul was able to not only think about his accomplishments, but he was concerned about his fellow Christians as well. Paul was concerned that he would live the kind of life that would encourage other Christians to be all they could be for Christ.

I live my life to encourage others to be all they can be in Christ.

"What you have learned and received and heard and seen in me - practice these things, and the God of peace will be with you" (Philippians 4:9).

- I live my life to encourage others to be all they can be in Christ.
- I say to others, "Keep putting into practice all you learned from me and saw me doing."
- If others follow my life, the God of peace will be with them.

CHRIST ACTUALIZATION CAN BE THE POSITION OF EVERY CHRISTIAN

In today's world, being self-actualized would seem to be the ultimate accomplishment. However, if we look closely at the above verses, we will see Paul was more than self-actualized, he was Christ-actualized. All of his goals were involved with his relationship with Christ. Christ was his source of strength and accomplishment.

If others copy my behavior God's peace will be with them.

Being Christ-actualized has to do with our position of right standing with God. When we receive Jesus Christ as our Savior, we are born again spiritually into God's family. As such, we are given a position of right standing with God. Right standing is what we are in Christ. It has nothing to do with what we do; rather it is based on what Jesus did for us at Calvary. Therefore, if you have Christ as Savior, you are a new creature or creation. Old things have passed away. All things are new and all things are of God. Again, this new creation is nothing that you did; it was completely done in you by God. We are told that *"For our sake he made him to be sin who knew no sin, so that in him we might become the righteousness of God"* (II Corinthians 5:21).

As children of God, through Jesus Christ, we are the righteousness of God Himself.

- I am the righteousness of God in Christ Jesus.

WE ARE CONTINUALLY IN THE PROCESS OF BECOMING

The late Dr. W. P. Rutledge shared an important insight into the growth process that we are all experiencing. He quoted from James Coleman's book, *Abnormal Psychology and Modern Life*, third edition. Coleman refers to a statement by C. R. Rogers.

> "The fully functioning person is constantly changing and developing. The process of becoming can take place only when the individual feels accepted, safe, and free to explore his innermost thoughts and feelings. This reveals a willingness to be a process. The individual accepts himself as continually in the process of becoming. Instead of striving to be a finished product, he continually tries to discover and actualize new aspects of himself in the course of living. The fully functioning person is one who frees himself from dependence on a social role, or conformity to the expectations of others, or cynical denial of deeper feelings. He becomes an existing, experiencing, emerging, growing, unique person."

Dr. Rutledge's comments are as follows:

> "I would relate this to Romans 7 and 8.
> Where it shows Paul as a powerful and
> complete spiritual, functioning person that is
> continuing to grow and develop. The Bible
> teaches, I believe, that as we die to self-
> actualization, putting off the old self (nature)
> with its needs and demands, we will become
> Christ-actualized, by putting on the new self,
> with the 'changing from glory unto glory,
> created in righteousness and true holiness' –
> 'growing in grace and in the knowledge of
> the Lord.' I am impressed with Rogers
> treatment of the, 'fully functioning person,
> constantly changing and developing,'
> however, I believe the Christian is realizing
> this in the strength of the Holy Spirit. For
> example, '...*your old life is now dead and gone.
> You are living a brand new kind of life that is
> continually learning more and more of what is right,
> and trying constantly to be more and more like
> Christ who created this new life within you.*'
> (Colossians 3:9-10 TLB) This compares with
> Rogers - "The individual accepts himself as
> continually in the process of becoming.
> Instead of striving to be a finished product,
> he continually tries to discover and actualize
> new aspects of himself in the course of
> living."

The sad but true picture is that man can only go so far in his own becoming... the Christian denies himself to become like Christ, which is God Himself, the apex of "becoming!" The Apostle Paul wrote to the Philippians regarding this "high calling of God." In verses 3:12–16, he had not attained his goal of apprehending the glory of Christ, but he was *"Pressing on toward the mark for the prize of the high calling of God in Christ Jesus."* Paul was *"changing from glory to glory, by the Spirit of the Lord."* Therefore, in a sense, as Rogers said, "This individual accepts himself as continually in the process of becoming." It is still worthy of note that God is just as concerned for the process as well as for the finished product.

CHRIST GAVE THE BELIEVERS HIS POWER OF ATTORNEY

We are Christ-actualized when we conform to His image. In other words, we are Christ-actualized when we imitate Him. We are allowing Christ to live His life in and through us. We are daily striving to do our best at everything in order to bring glory and honor to our Lord. We have no need to seek rewards, for they are already there; they belong to us and they are beyond measure.

Jesus has all authority in heaven and earth, and He gave us His authority over all the power of the enemy. In Christ, we have regained our position of dominion on earth.

I run with patience the race that God has set before me. Then Jesus told us to occupy until He returns so we are to reign as "Kings of Life."

As Christians, we don't need to be motivated by fear of loss or punishment, nor do we need to aspire for recognition or reward. Instead we are inspired to be overcomers in Christ Jesus. We have Christ's authority to overcome the Prince of this evil world.

Jesus gave us His power of attorney to use His name to take full charge over the circumstances of our life. Now as we read this, hear this, when we believe this, and begin to live using the authority He has given us: "We can be anything we want to be." We can do anything we want to do, in and through Christ to His honor and glory.

The fourth Personal Characteristic of a Godly Life, "Being Christ-Actualized," shows us that our motivation to achieve comes from God's Word. We have displaced the negative programming of our past with positive acknowledgments based on His Word. We are overcomers by the full authority of Jesus's Name. *I am Christ actualized not self-actualized.*

I am a Christ-oriented personality and I am an overcomer-type person who is motivated by His love. I take Jesus's place and use Jesus's name just as though Jesus Himself were here. The only difference is that, instead of Jesus doing it Himself, He is living His life in and through me. I am acting at His command.

Chapter Twelve

FULFILLING SELF ESTEEM AND SELF ACTUALATION NEEDS

Questions for home study and group discussion

What is Paul's attitude about his walk with Christ?
I Corinthians 11:1

How did Paul use Jesus's example of how we are to live?
Hebrews 12:1–2

What did Paul consider necessary for him to experience
God's power?   Philippians 3:7–9

What did Paul say that would indicate he was more than
self-actualized?   Philippians 4:9, 13

What level can we achieve that is better than self-
actualization? II Corinthians 5:21
(What is this called in the text?)

Notes from My Mentor's Personal Experiences

_____
_____
_____
_____
_____
_____
_____
_____
_____
_____
_____
_____
_____
_____
_____
_____
_____
_____
_____
_____
_____
_____
_____
_____
_____
_____

Scripture Memory Chapter Twelve

"I can do all things through him who strengthens me." (Philippians 4:13)

FOUR PERSONAL CHARACTERISTICS OF A GODLY LIFE

PERSONAL CHARACTERISTIC ONE

BEING PHYSICALLY PURE

I honor God with every part of my body

PERSONAL CHARACTERISTIC TWO

BEING LOVE MOTIVATED

I love my family more than I love myself

PERSONAL CHARACTERISTIC THREE

BEING EXTREMELY VALUED

I know and love who I am in Christ;
I am a person of extreme value

PERSONAL CHARACTERISTIC FOUR

BEING CHRIST ACTUALIZED

I am Christ-actualized rather than self-actualized

ABOUT THE AUTHOR

D r. Roy Comstock is the author of *Mentoring His Way, Disciple Twelve*, covering the "Twelve Characteristics of a Godly Life". He and his wife Sarah co-founded the Christian Mentors Network in 2000.

Roy is a man who has had many unique life experiences. In his early childhood days, he was forced to adapt to living in fourteen different foster homes. As an ambitious businessman, he saw the rise and fall of his own multimillion-dollar corporation, which led to the humbling adjustment of a life in prison confinement. This was a lesson in what can happen to a Christian who dares to take their eyes off Jesus for a time.

This book has not been written by a perfect man or by one whose life has always been a model for others to follow. Roy's life has not always been easy. He, like all true Christians, has been and is a work of God "in process." We may call this Roy Comstock's "Prison Epistle," since much of this material was written while he was serving a prison term.

Roy experienced major failure to his marriage, his business, and his personal life because of his misguided focus on self rather than on Christ. But Roy repented and turned to Christ in a deeper way than ever before. He cried out to the Lord concerning his own life, and the Lord responded not only to his needs, but also taught him insights that can be of great help to anyone who desires to truly follow Jesus Christ. It was during his time in prison that the Lord revealed many of the principles that Roy calls the "Twelve Characteristics of a Godly Life."

Roy and his wife Sarah, live in Valencia, California. www.christianmentorsnetwork.org

Made in the USA
Coppell, TX
24 February 2021